Time Management for Women

Simple Productivity Strategies to Get More Stuff Done in Less Time for Work-Life Balance and Stress-Free Living

Claire Haven

Table of Contents

Introduction

Everyone gets the same amount of time in a day, yet it can feel harder for you to manage your time than most people. This is not a strange occurrence; many women feel this on a daily basis. From waking up and rushing to work and then coming home to clean up around the house and cook for your family, you likely have a lot on your plate. When you don't know how to manage your time, fitting all of these tasks in a day seems impossible and stressful. If you can identify with this sentiment, you are likely a woman with too much to do and not enough resources to make it happen.

When it comes to time, there is no way to make more of it. What must happen is a complete prioritization of all the tasks that you must accomplish each day. By changing the way you view your schedule, you will realize that the time you have can work for you. Once you are able to do this, the problems that once held you back will merely be steps to take toward living your most productive life.

The statistics are surprising — with only 10 minutes of planning each day, this can save you up to two hours of time spent trying to get organized. A lot of time is wasted when you try to make your plan right before you complete your tasks. Your plan is something that should be created ahead of time, giving you the advantage of being one step ahead of what you are trying to accomplish.

Only 10% of what you read is retained the first time. The retention rate of an action that is done is 90%. A staggering difference, this proves that the more you practice productivity, the more that the habit will be retained. While you can go over your plan as much as necessary, the most important part is that you are applying the action that is necessary to follow through.

The solution to having better time management skills does not involve a total renovation of your lifestyle. All it takes is knowing how to kick-start your brain into thinking productively. By giving yourself the motivation necessary to keep moving, you will find it a very positive experience when you can check something off your to-do list. From going to bed earlier to working in a quiet space, these are small steps that can be taken that will make a huge difference in your ability to manage your time.

Having a backup plan is also essential. While you can plan for the things that you expect throughout the day, you cannot predict what others will say or do. This is why staying flexible is also an essential part of practicing productivity. If something changes at the last minute, you should still be able to remain efficient throughout your day. This guide is going to teach you all of the skills that you will need in order to be an expert at utilizing your time wisely.

As a busy woman myself, time management is a topic that is familiar and prominent. Feeling disappointed because there are still tasks left on the to-do list at the end of the day is a struggle that we all face. This struggle can turn into a passion that will guide you toward better habits and newfound knowledge about what it takes to be the best version of yourself that you can be.

I used to struggle with time management because I would take on too much at once, expecting myself to complete each and every single task that I laid out for myself. As soon as I realized organization and prioritization can make all the difference, I was left feeling that I could tackle anything I set my mind to.

While finding ways to motivate myself, I was able to stay on track and focus on the goals that I set for myself. There was no more wallowing in disappointment or feeling that the list is never going to end. This is possible for you too. A desire to make a change is the first sign that you have what it takes in order to better manage your time.

Once you discover that you already have everything that you need in order to become better with managing your time, you will notice an immediate rise in your self-confidence. When you feel good about yourself and your abilities, you are less likely to let any doubts hold you back. Knowing that you are capable of the goals that you set is a very empowering feeling.

Other people are going to take notice of your confidence too. It is hard not to because having a healthy sense of confidence is contagious. Everything in your life is going to have a meaning and a purpose. When you become great at making a schedule, there is nothing that will be left unaccounted for. Your aim will be to assign each task a purpose that makes sense in your life. When you can see how each action is going to impact you directly, it truly opens your eyes and allows you to stay with these positive habits.

Women who have used these methods are still well on their paths to success. Most women agree that it was a lot easier than they thought it would be; the hardest part is getting started with productivity. Once this has been accomplished, it becomes easier as time goes on.

Many women have also seen improvements in their personal lives that were a direct result of following these methods. It is a lot easier to be present for your loved ones and friends when you aren't focused on all of the things that you must do. These methods are going to give you a way to assign time to get everything done, personal tasks included. You will find that you do not need to give up the things that you love doing just because you have responsibilities. With effective time management strategies in place, you will be able to do everything without having to make any sacrifices.

By the time you are through reading this guide, you are going to feel empowered and ready to take on any task that comes your way. Not only will you have the ability to accomplish the things that are currently on your to-do list, but you will be able to flawlessly incorporate new things onto the list as well. You will realize that there is nothing too difficult to accomplish as long as you are aware of how to approach it.

By utilizing your determination, motivation, and patience, you will wonder why you didn't try these methods sooner. Having this knowledge is powerful, and it is important that you use this power toward productivity. Don't stop after your first day of success; keep the momentum going so that you can create great habits for life.

Waiting until the "right time" to start implementing these strategies is not going to bring you success. The fact is, there is no time that is more right than others. The best time to begin is right now because you will have to learn how to incorporate these time management skills into your current schedule. Procrastination is only going to enforce your lazy habits, which will lead you to a much harder time mastering productive habits.

If you truly care to make a change, you will know that starting immediately is the best way to immerse yourself in these methods. By utilizing these step-by-step techniques, even the busiest women will have time to take care of their responsibilities while still paying attention to the rest of their physical and emotional needs. Whether you are a mother, a working professional, or both, this guide is going to show you that time management is possible during any stage.

Chapter 1: Getting Started with Time Management for Women

Chapter 1: Getting Started with Time Management for Women

Imagine your average day at work — the struggle to wake up on time, how hard it is to leave your house while ensuring that you have everything that you need to get through your day. Once you arrive at work, the race begins. You are answering phone calls, catching up on emails, and managing the constant stack of paperwork that sits on the edge of your desk.

Alongside all of this, your boss keeps coming into your office, asking if you have finished your tasks yet, or provides you with even more that must be done before the end of the day. Occasionally, you will get a visit from a coworker that distracts you from the overwhelming workload that stares you down. This is how stress is created, and you have likely experienced a day very similar to this one. In fact, this is an average day for most women in the workplace.

The day doesn't end here — it is only halfway over. After you finish your stressful day at work, you must go home to complete your remaining responsibilities. This can look like anything from making dinner to getting the children ready for bed. You must also maintain the cleanliness of your house while trying to figure out when to squeeze in some quality time with your spouse.

The thought of trying to get this all done is enough to add even more stress to your day than what you already took on at work. Once nighttime comes, this is your chance to relax and unwind. As you are trying to do this in bed, you might come to the realization that you have work in only a few hours and that this is a vicious cycle with no end in sight.

Wishing that you have more time in a day comes naturally when you are living your life as the above example is portrayed. What many women fail to realize is that there are solutions to this problem. In fact, there are many solutions that you can begin using right now.

A major issue that stems from not having any time management strategies throughout your day is that you begin to feel guilty for not being able to spend as much time with your loved ones as you should. Quality time is important, and it is not something that you should need to eliminate altogether in order to feel like you can accomplish all of your tasks.

One survey reveals that 39% of working mothers admit that they feel they do not spend enough time with their children. From this same survey, 41% of working mothers said that being a parent actually makes it more difficult for them to advance in areas of work.

This displays that there is a clear imbalance between personal time and work time, as a large percentage of women are feeling this way despite what they do for a living. Not being able to determine what areas of your life should be prioritized can cause a real problem between that personal and work balance. This is another reason why there is no better time than right now to begin with some time management strategies.

The Shift to a Solution

Dwelling on an issue is never going to change its outcome. While it is important for you to allow yourself to feel emotions, it is just as important to figure out how you are going to move forward. Time management is defined by your ability to plan out the way you are going to allocate your time. What you must realize is that it is possible to control this aspect of your schedule.

This is not a new concept; time management has been utilized since the late 1800s. Frederick Winslow Taylor is considered to be the man who conceptualized time management. In 1911, he wrote a book titled *The Principles of Scientific Time Management*. This started a movement of utilizing time efficiently and controlling what we spend our time on in a given day.

Taylor believed that, in order to see results, you must standardize the way that you complete your tasks. From farming to cooking dinner, creating a method in which you utilize certain steps will allow you to complete all your tasks in a uniform fashion. Today, we have even more resources available to us.

With the use of technology, you are able to complete certain tasks in minutes that would've taken hours or even days just decades ago. It is important to realize that you do have several resources that are available to you right now. Even just utilizing your phone calendar in order to keep track of your schedule is going to help you more than trying to remember everything in your head.

Instead of being unable to sleep at night because you are worried about how you are going to get everything done, you can become an empowered woman who chooses to take control over the time that you are given. When you see how much all of the resources and tips can assist you, it will give you the necessary boost of confidence in order to keep going.

The sooner that you are able to begin, the sooner that your life is going to become more efficient. By utilizing these methods, you will likely notice several aspects of your life improve (even those you didn't know required improvement). Know that there is always room for improvement, even on the smallest scale. These nuances make a difference in the bigger picture of your life.

Why You Should Start Managing Your Time

Everyone wants to eliminate stress in their lives, and becoming great at time management will do just that. Instead of spending your time being stressed out over things that you think you can't control, change your perspective to realize that there is always something that can be done to make your life easier.

Once you get the hang of time management, you will see that you have even more time than you realized. With this freedom, you will be able to accomplish additional tasks that you probably hadn't even thought of when you were stuck feeling overwhelmed.

Aside from the practicality of it all, you will also have more time to spend doing the things that you love. Spending time with your loved ones should definitely be made a priority in your life. These emotional bonds are essential to your happiness, and you deserve to experience them.

When you enter with the mindset that you aren't going to sacrifice these moments just because you have a to-do list to take care of, you will see that you are more likely to be able to figure out a way to manage your time better. Start your day knowing that you plan to complete an equal amount to social time.

When you have less stress in your life, you will notice a physical difference. Too much stress has the ability to lead to anxiety disorders, even depression. It is not something that should be continually overlooked just because you feel that it is what you have to do. Since there is always another method that you can try, continue to experiment until you find the time-saving techniques that fit best in your life.

You will also have more energy and stamina to get through your day, allowing you to feel productive. It can be easy to become reclusive once you have finished up with all your responsibilities, especially when you are spreading yourself thin. Your goal is still to be able to enjoy your life while also living as efficiently as possible.

The Causes of Lost Time

1. Focusing on one task

If you have 10 tasks that you must accomplish in a day, it doesn't make sense to focus on one only. When you do this, you are putting yourself in the position to become stressed out, especially if the task is particularly challenging. By only putting effort into a single task, the effort is wasted by the end of the day. When the next day comes, you are going to have all 10 of those tasks that you did not finish, plus any additional ones.

Solution: Give yourself a time limit on how much

energy you are going to put into each task. If something is too difficult or requires something additional to finish it, then move on to the next thing that you are able to complete. Sometimes, when you work this way, you will be able to finish things once you step away from them and then return to them. A fresh perspective is always helpful and encouraging.

2. Not sticking to your schedule

A schedule is useless if you do not abide by it. When you put in the effort to create your schedule, you need to make sure that you also follow through with it. One of the hardest things to do is to follow a schedule that you set for yourself, but it is a necessary part of becoming great with time management.

Solution: Include basic things on your schedule, such as driving to work and cooking dinner. When you see that you are actually accomplishing these things on time, you will feel more motivated to complete the other tasks. The more that you can make scheduling a habit, the easier it will be to follow through with it.

3. Lack of prioritizing

Maybe you are able to accomplish some things, yet you feel that you still do not have time for the deadlines that matter most. This has everything to do with prioritization. As you are checking things off your to-do list, you need to make sure that the most important ones are being prioritized.

Solution: The easiest way to prioritize is to take a look at all of your tasks written down. From there, mark a star next to each one that has a deadline. After you have these tasks separated from the rest, you can prioritize even further by listing them in order of importance.

4. Giving in to laziness

It can feel incredibly nice to relax when you are feeling tired and overwhelmed. We all need this time to unwind, but it is important that you are reasonable with it. If you decide to sit back and watch TV before you have accomplished any of your tasks, it is unlikely that you are going to get up and do them afterward. Laziness should be treated as a reward.

Solution: Only allow yourself to be lazy after you have done everything productive that you can do at that moment. It becomes too difficult to switch back and forth between restful and productive, so it is best that you do not try to force yourself to do this. When you are able to rest, it is going to feel so much more justified and satisfactory.

Overview

With the use of the methods that will be discussed throughout this guide, you are going to be able to take control over the time that you have to work with. Starting from the very first steps of effective time management, the habits that you create for yourself are going to help you stay on track and in control. Instead of wondering why you keep running out of time, you are going to find viable solutions that you can apply to your life immediately.

Instead of struggling to catch up during your daily tasks, you are going to be a step ahead. After identifying what causes you to lose time throughout your day, you are going to create a plan that is customized to work with your lifestyle. There will be nothing that is too far out of reach.

As a busy woman, you already have enough to worry

about. Running out of time should not be an additional worry on that list. Once you master these new skills, you will have what it takes to continue each day going forward with a productive schedule in place. This allows you to be your most confident self.

By banishing procrastination and creating new habits, there is no reason that you will ever have to fall victim to laziness again. No matter where you are or what you are doing, this guide is going to provide you with practical solutions that you can apply. There will be no more room for excuses as to why your tasks did not get accomplished on the first try.

Aside from taking care of your responsibilities, you will also learn how to make time for yourself. This is an equally important step to becoming self-sufficient. When you are able to find this balance, you can successfully say that you have mastered the art of time management.

Quick Start Action Step

Something that you can do right now is to download a great calendar app to your phone. As suggested, this is a way that you can get a jumpstart on your productivity. There are several different apps that you can utilize, so download one that you feel will best fit your needs.

If you already have an app like this, utilize it even more. Make an effort to import all your tasks into this app so that you do not forget anything. Aside from being able to keep track of them all, you will also have a clear picture of the work that lies ahead for you.

When you write down your goals, they are more likely to be accomplished. The same can be said for keeping great time management habits. No matter how big or how small the task is, make sure that you are utilizing your calendar app to its fullest potential.

Chapter 2:
Why We Seem to
Lack Time

Chapter 2: Why We Seem to Lack Time

In this chapter, we are going to take a deeper look at why it is so easy to lose track of time. This is something universally felt by all women, regardless of the job they work or the schedule they keep. It is likely that this week already, you have experienced a lack of time. Did it make you feel overwhelmed? Did it add stress to your life?

By having a true understanding of how you let the time slip away from you, it becomes easier to identify a solution that will work. If you begin by applying every solution that you can think of, not only will the problem persist, but it is also harder to keep track of what is actually working.

Changing the way that you perceive your time is also an important step toward making the most of it. When you use phrases like "crunched for time" and "stretched thin," you are already insisting that time has control over you instead of the other way around. It is like admitting defeat before you even begin.

Consider using only positive language when you are

referring to time and your schedule. Instead of thinking about your day as a big pressured event where you must cram everything in, think about how you are going to finish your to-do list and then indulge in something that you enjoy. When you have something to look forward to, you will be a lot more motivated to work.

Sometimes, it isn't even your responsibilities that take up most of your time. Consider the things that you do not actually *have* to do. Being overbearing is a natural habit that many women have because it is within their nature to help. Know that you can only control so much of what goes on. Allow your children to learn and explore while having the confidence that your spouse can also navigate through their own issues. Realize that your coworkers need to be responsible on their own.

Letting go of the idea that you must fix everything is going to create a lot more time in your day. While it is still kind to be helpful and available, you will be able to relocate this time toward the tasks that you have that aren't getting finished. Once these tasks are done, then you can check if there is anything more that you can do for others.

When you are able to let go and focus on the things that require your effort, you won't feel like you are running a marathon just to get through a single day. You should be able to control the general feeling that surrounds your own day. If you wake up in a good mood, then there are ways that you can ensure you will stay in a good mood, even if you encounter difficult tasks along the way.

Below, we are going to look even further into some of the causes of lost time:

1. Stress

No matter what you are doing each day, if you harbor any kind of stress for a long period of time, this is going to make you less productive. It becomes a vicious cycle because you will see that you are losing time, but you will still feel unable to do something about it.

Being stagnant when you have a lot to do is like a magnet for stressful situations. You are opening yourself up to the feeling and acting in a vulnerable way that won't benefit you in the future. Once you do finally start to take action, you are going to have to play catch-up.

Knowing that you can handle stress is a great feeling. It is not something that needs to take over your life. Before you give in and think that there is nothing else that can be done, consider taking a few deep breaths and stepping away from your task. Most of the time, this is a very refreshing action that can help you to overcome the stress.

2. Never-ending lists

Utilizing a to-do list is supposed to be a helpful way for you to stay on track. When you create a to-do list for yourself, consider only planning on listing the items that are due each day. If you keep working off the same list, it is going to feel like you will never reach its end.

Some tasks will be carried over to your next list, but try to shift your focus only to what is in front of you at the moment. Since you are prioritizing each to-do list, you shouldn't be missing any tasks. At the end of each day, you can observe which items need to be worked on a bit more.

Having a to-do list with no end not only damages you emotionally, but it can also cause you to think that you do not have any leisure time. This is what causes you to put off spending time with loved ones and practicing self-care. At the end of each day, you should be able to put your list away and recharge instead of thinking about it all through the night.

3. Working during downtime

When you are relaxing, you should only be focusing on relaxing. This works the same way as when you are focusing on your work. If you are distracted by the things that you still have to do, you aren't going to be able to unwind properly.

Consider what you are actually doing during your leisure time. Just because you aren't working on your to-do list doesn't mean you won't unintentionally take on someone else's. For example, when you spend time with your spouse, don't spend this time helping them complete a task on their list. Your time should be spent doing something that allows you to enjoy each other's company.

The same concept can be applied to spending time with your friends. When you are helping a friend move, this isn't exactly the best option for unwinding. Your brain is still activated, and you are focused on a particular task. Meeting a friend for lunch would be a more appropriate example of truly enjoying your free time.

Make sure that you are also utilizing your lunch break for its intended purpose. It can be tempting to try to get ahead with your work while you are eating, but this takes away from the time that you can spend clearing your mind. When you do this, it is like you never get a break.

4. Unattainable goals

You need to be reasonable with the goals that you set for yourself. You would never sit your child down in front of a quantum physics book and expect them to pick up all of the concepts in one sitting, so why should you expect the same from yourself when you set a bunch of unrealistic goals?

You need to keep this in mind as you make your to-do list. Truly ask yourself if the expectations that you are placing on yourself are going to be met with a successful end result. Sure, your goals will probably challenge you, but they shouldn't leave you feeling frustrated and disappointed.

The more that you work with time management, the more you will know what your particular boundaries are. These boundaries differ for everyone. We are all equipped with different skills and abilities to handle different kinds of stressors. If you make a goal for yourself that you know will only stress you out, consider breaking it down into smaller steps.

5. Lack of fun

Even while you are getting work done, you should still be able to find humor in the situation. Being able to breathe and even smile is going to help you out tremendously. When you are working on difficult tasks, make sure that you take the time to remember what you are thankful for. Whether you would like to look at a picture of your family or watch a video of your pet, do whatever it takes to lighten the mood.

You need to acknowledge the fact that you are only going to be able to focus on something serious for a certain amount of time. Things can happen during your day that will cause your mood to fluctuate. If you have ever tried to complete your to-do list while you are in a bad mood, then you know how true this is.

Know that being in control is not always equivalent to being happy. Think about the things that make you the happiest and see if there is a way that you can incorporate more of these things throughout your day. Just as you might encounter hurdles, when you are able to encounter these small bursts of joy, your mood is going to reflect this greatly.

Taking a break to have a conversation about something that isn't related to the work you are doing can benefit you. As long as you are able to keep this quick and concise, it should not hinder you by providing a distraction. Even when you are taking breaks, your time management skills are going to be essential.

Why Identification of Lost Time Is Important

The reason you must be aware of where your lost time has gone is simple — you will be able to identify what areas you must work on in order to manage your time better. There comes a sense of acceptance when you are able to see the habits that could use improvement and visualize how much better your life is going to be once you change them.

You must be very honest with yourself as you are working through this step. If you continually make excuses for your behavior, then nothing is ever going to change. As long as you have the desire to better manage your time and the right attitude, then you will be met with success for your efforts.

Because the process of time management can be accomplished by taking smaller steps, accepting yourself and your habits can be enough motivation to get you started. Taking a look at your biggest problems and turning them into strengths is a very admirable trait to have.

You will be able to see the bigger, clearer picture once you determine the habits that are holding you back. We all have them, so there is no need for you to feel down or to punish yourself over them. The only productive step is to accept them and to keep moving forward. This allows true change to begin in your life.

Quick Start Action Step

Now that you have a broader sense of some ways that time can be lost, review the examples in this chapter and the previous one. Write down all of the things that apply to you and to your life right now. There is no right or wrong answer. Don't think too hard about it. Simply write it down if it applies to you in any way.

Once you are able to see a concrete list of these things that challenge you, this means that you know exactly what you need to work on. From here, you can formulate the steps that you must take. It can be an eye-opening experience to see exactly what is holding you back.

By looking at this list, you should feel excited about the changes that are about to take place. Don't let it bring you down or make you feel like a failure. Remember, everyone has flaws that they would like to change. By taking a proactive approach, you are going to be doing everything that you can in order to make those changes a reality.

Seeing these things in writing helps to take away their power over you. Instead of being intimidated, you can channel this energy into one that allows you to feel motivated. Some of the most powerful women in the world have gone through these same obstacles, and they were able to overcome them because of their desire to become better at time management.

Allow yourself to believe that you can follow the same path too. The things that once challenged you are going to become nothing more than old habits. It is amazing what you are capable of once you truly put your mind toward changing your behavior for the better.

Chapter 3: Understanding Time Management (Shifting Your Mindset)

Chapter 3: Understanding Time Management (Shifting Your Mindset)

The way that you think holds a tremendous amount of power. It is your mindset that tells you whether you believe in yourself or not. Your mindset shapes the person that you are and allows you to feel either determined or discouraged. Think about the way that you treat yourself.

If you are constantly pointing out your own flaws, this is not doing anything for your self-esteem except for breaking it down. You are the one person that you can always rely on, so do your best to build yourself up. Allow yourself to feel proud of your accomplishments. It is not wrong to celebrate your victories.

Becoming great at time management is a long-term process. If you plan on seeing long-term results, then you must be prepared for this process by understanding it as best as you can. It is not necessarily going to be hard to incorporate the steps into your current lifestyle, but changing your way of thinking can prove to be challenging.

This change in your mindset is necessary if you hope to see positive results. You cannot realistically expect yourself to be great at time management when you are doubtful of your own abilities. From this moment on, only speak to yourself using positive reinforcements. If you mess up, use it as a learning experience instead of a chance to participate in self-loathing — for example, "I didn't organize my entire closet, but I was able to get rid of all the things that I no longer use in order to make more space."

You must be able to recognize the small things that you accomplish because these small things eventually lead to or become a part of bigger ones. Once you realize how much happier you are when you can go with the flow, it will become natural to respond to things in a positive manner going forward.

Have you ever noticed how much easier it is to get things done when you are in a good mood? When you feel good about yourself, you are naturally going to feel more confident. If you aren't in a good mood, it becomes easier to doubt yourself or become discouraged before you even begin.

What to Remember

1. Manage your emotions.

As you become better at changing your mindset, you will also naturally become better at managing your emotions. The emotions that you portray play a large role in your success. Not only is emotional control important for successful time management skills, but it is also essential for your happiness.

Certain situations are going to lead you to certain emotions. If you get a promotion, you feel joyful. If your car breaks down, you will feel stressed. Being able to process your emotions is an important part of living a healthy life, no matter what lifestyle you choose.

It is natural for you to want to be in control of your emotions, yet you might not know how to separate them from the stressors that you encounter. By changing your mindset, you are opening your way of thinking. Instead of being hindered by the challenges you face, you can turn them into lessons that you can learn from.

Becoming someone who can look at the "bright side" of all situations is a way to promote a positive mindset. It might seem pointless to you at first, but once you begin the practice, you will see that the things that once really bothered you are easier to overcome.

Instead of becoming paralyzed with negative emotions, you must learn how to turn inward. While bad things might be happening around you (and even to you), they aren't going to last forever. There are always solutions that you can apply or things that you can do differently to impact the outcome that you face.

It makes much more sense to process your feelings and then continue forward with a solution than to let the negativity take over your life. This is definitely easier said than done, but this is why you need to turn looking for the bright side of things into a daily habit.

Like any habit, it is going to take some time for it to become permanent. You must learn how to retrain your mind after all of the months or years of looking at things a certain way. Instead of looking at your schedule and thinking that there's no way you can get it done, you will be able to see it as a structure to follow.

2. Develop self-esteem.

There are many things that you will face that will cause you to question your belief in yourself. Maybe you are finding parenting to be difficult, always having to disciple your child, or maybe you feel that your partner does not see you as good enough because you don't spend enough time together.

There are countless things that can cause you to question your ability to be successful, but this does not mean that they have to hinder you. Separate the way that you feel about yourself with the way that you *think* others feel about you. Do the things that you know you are good at, and feel proud of yourself for doing them.

When you have low self-esteem, it is important that you set yourself up for success in order to build it up. Starting from the way that you talk about yourself, you have the ability to change your inner dialogue. Once you are able to see yourself in a positive light, it becomes much easier to see other situations in this way.

Gravitate toward the things and the people that inspire you. When you feel inspired, you are going to act more passionately. It becomes easy to get stuck in a rut when you don't know what you actually enjoy doing. Try your best to incorporate some of these things into your daily life.

Allow yourself to recognize the strengths that you have. There are countless ways for you to celebrate these strengths while practicing them daily. For example, if you have a nurturing personality, you can let it shine. Whether you are at work or at home with your family, allow your nurturing side to come through by being an empathetic individual. People are going to take notice, and you will feel great doing it.

3. Look toward success.

When you are unsure about your mindset, it might be difficult to imagine yourself being successful. The doubts start to form, and you begin to second-guess yourself. Doing some research on the successful people that you admire most can prove to be very beneficial.

When you model your mindset after the habits of those who are already successful, you can imagine that the same principles will apply to your own life. A change in perspective is sometimes all it takes for you to see that a change is possible within your own life too.

Being more of an optimist means that you are more likely going to think about winning ideas. You should feel inspired and motivated at all times, despite any hardships that you are going through. It is a complete transformation of the way that you view your life and your surrounds.

Pay attention to the people that you are spending time around. Would you classify them as mostly optimistic people? You must make sure that the energy around you matches the energy that you would like to project. Naturally, we tend to take on the energy of those who are frequently around us.

If you find that there is someone or something in your life that is bringing you down and preventing you from living as an optimist, then you might need to make a change. Spend less time with that person or in that type of situation. If you cannot, then think about ways to protect yourself and your spirit.

4. Harness drive.

Your drive is the force that allows you to feel

motivated in the things that you do. Sometimes, it can feel like you are running on empty when you are trying to tackle the various things on your schedule. At certain points throughout the week, you might even feel like you can't push forward any longer.

Use your drive to keep you going. With a mindset that is optimistic and full of motivational tools, you should find it easier to feel driven. Even when you are simply making your family dinner after a long day, thinking about the nutrition that you are providing them could be a driving force to allow you to enjoy cooking the meal.

Drive has a lot to do with gratitude. Tasks can be bothersome, even if they help you accomplish the things that you want to do. Being grateful for what you have is a way to reel back the feelings of stress. Instead of being bummed out that you have to get up early for work, consider that a little bit of additional hard work can result in a promotion with more freedom. This is one of many examples that might apply to your life right now.

Make it a point to consider what you are thankful for on a regular basis. This is going to keep you feeling grounded and stable. You will have a clear image in your mind of what you are working toward, and sometimes that is all it takes to feel recharged and ready to take on the tasks ahead.

5. Tackle adversity.

No matter what you are trying to accomplish, you are bound to run into some form of adversity along the way. In order to get through these rough parts, it is important that you have a strong mindset. This is going to keep you from becoming upset with yourself or with the situation at hand.

Adversity is normally anything that makes you feel like you cannot complete a task. Whether it is intentional or unintentional, it can lead you to believe that you aren't good enough to reach your goals. Having a strong mindset is important for overcoming these issues.

When you are able to be flexible with changes that are outside of your control, it becomes a lot easier to handle them. Accept the fact that you can only control your own actions sometimes, and that is enough. If you are doing your best, you should not feel that you have to punish yourself or put yourself down.

If you have ever been working on something and been completely derailed, then it is likely that you have experienced adversity. What comes next is the choice that you must make; you must decide how you are going to deal with it.

Generally, you have two options — rise above or succumb to the things that try to delay your progress. Being able to let go of your original plan and to focus on a new one can feel like a failure at first. What you must remember is that there are several ways for you to reach the same end result.

With many of these steps, the more that you practice acting in this mindset, the more natural that they become. You will see that your resilience will begin to take control, even when you feel that you have no control. Even when you feel that you have several impossible tasks at hand, if you take a deep breath and regroup your thoughts, you would be amazed at the progress that you can make.

Getting outside can be helpful. When you remove yourself from whatever working environment that you are in, this provides your brain with a chance to reset itself. Taking short breaks as you are working toward a goal can be enough to allow you to think outside of the box for alternative solutions.

Stress relief tools are also a great option. Anything that allows you to fidget or think about something else is the perfect way to make sure that you are staying within your positive mindset. Even just a short conversation with someone about a different topic can provide the same effect.

Steps to Take

Much like you will learn as you study more about the topic of time management, tasks are easier done when there are smaller steps involved. These small steps will lead you to the final goal without any added stress or pressure. You will feel as if you are able to accomplish anything as long as you are able to determine what steps you must take. The following are the steps for you to take as you work on changing your mindset:

1. Change the way you talk to yourself.
2. Make sure you are using positive language.
3. Determine what you would like your mindset to

be.

4. Study the topic and apply what you learn.
5. Spend time with those who reflect your desired mindset.
6. Create habits that support your new mindset.
7. Step outside of your comfort zone.

In a few steps, you will be able to transform the way you think. You might be able to accomplish some of these things fairly quickly, while others you will need to spend more time on. There is no time limit on your success when it comes to changing your mindset, but the sooner that you can get it done, the better. When you have these new skills and a more positive way of thinking, you are going to be able to apply them toward becoming better at time management.

Quick Start Action Step

For this step, you are going to pick a time when you plan on going through all of the processes above that are involved with changing your mindset. Remember, it is always possible for you to make time for the things that are important to you. Make sure that you are prioritizing your change in mindset.

It sounds simple, and that's because it is! Making a commitment is a sign that you are going to be great at managing your time. When committing to changing your mindset, think about it as a part of the bigger picture. You are instantly going to feel happier and better, but it is also going to help you when you go through some of your biggest time management struggles.

No one else is going to be able to fit this task onto your schedule except for you. This is a true test of your ability to follow through for yourself. Think about how much you want this change, and let the desire motivate you to work hard.

Chapter 4: Setting Priorities for Achievable Goals

Chapter 4: Setting Priorities for Achievable Goals

So far, you have a lot of new concepts to think about. You have already explored the importance of learning how your time is lost, and you know how to get in a better mindset. Now, you must focus on prioritizing your goals in order to make sure that they are achievable.

As mentioned, you never want to make goals for yourself that will set you up for failure. Not only is this extremely discouraging, but it is also a big waste of time. Be smart about your goals and the things that you truly need to accomplish. Know that you have the ability to decide which ones you should work on first.

When you have a lot to do, it can seem like everything needs all of your attention at once. This isn't the case, though. Utilizing your prioritization skills will help you see that you do have choices when it comes to what must be done first. Anything that you make a priority is something that is most important to you.

Priorities are usually determined by deadlines and

general categories. For example, a doctor's appointment is naturally going to take priority over buying a new rug for the living room to replace your old one. Health and wellness should always come first, followed by work and school.

Anything that is a priority is something that cannot or should not be rescheduled unless there is a very good reason for doing so. These are the most important tasks for you to not procrastinate on. Not only will this set you back on your schedule, but you might also end up missing the important deadlines that have been set.

When you spend time putting off any task, this means that you are going to have to take up even more time than you originally would have if you had just completed the task in the beginning. When you think about it this way, you'll also realize that your other tasks are going to be neglected because you will have to split your time between them and the things that you have been putting off.

Prioritization makes your path clear. You will always know what is coming next, and you will feel good about getting tasks completed on schedule. Each goal that you accomplish is going to motivate you to complete the next one on the list. This becomes a great habit that pays off.

Write Things Down

It is known that writing something down is an additional way for you to remember to do it. The more senses that you utilize, the greater the chance that you are going to get it done. When you practice the habit of writing things down, you are embedding the information into your conscious and subconscious.

When you can remember that you have tasks to do, this will guide you toward proactive steps. This is what it takes in order to see results. Vowing that you are going to change your mindset is only the beginning of what great time management can do for you and your life.

1. Awareness of time: When you have your tasks written down, you will get to see a clear picture of how much time you need to spend on each one. If you know that you have two hours of free time each day with 10 tasks to complete, careful distribution is going to be a necessity.

2. *Automatic organization:* When you write something down versus simply recalling it from memory, you are acting in a more organized fashion. Even if your goals aren't prioritized yet, they are in the same place for you to refer to. It can be very easy to forget about tasks or deadlines when you are going through several other things each day.

3. *Constant reminders:* When you are able to see your tasks written out, this serves as a reminder of the things that you must accomplish. Suppressing becomes a common habit when you tend to lean on procrastination as a crutch. Writing things down eliminates this habit for you. It forces you to take a look at all that is expected of you in that given moment.

4. *Boost in mood:* When your mind isn't clouded with all of the things that you must do, you have more time to enjoy your life. You will feel that you are able to breathe without the whole weight of the world upon your shoulders. Allocating your tasks to paper is a great way to regroup your thoughts and reel in your focus.

5. *Easy to compare:* When you need to coordinate your schedule with someone else's, it is important that you are able to access your own quickly and efficiently. Whether you prefer to manually write your schedule down or utilize a digital app, there should be a way for you to reference it and access it easily.

Steps to Take

1. Merge your plan and your calendar. It is great to have a plan, but without a calendar to keep track of your schedule, it is unlikely that you are going to make great use out of that plan. The same can be said for when you have a calendar but no plan. You must have both in order to succeed.

Much like any goal that you have made in the past to make your life better, this also needs to be backed by actions that match the end result. You cannot just expect these changes to happen without any effort on your behalf. Think about prioritization and goal-setting in the same context.

2. Set boundaries for yourself: It can be hard to balance personal life with responsibilities. With all of the distractions that are available at your fingertips, you might struggle with when it is time to work and when it is time to relax. As stated, both are equally important in time management strategies.

In order to make sure that you are abiding by some sort of guidelines, time yourself when you are taking personal time in between tasks. There is no need to do this at the end of your day when you are ready to permanently unwind, but it is a good idea for when you aren't finished working yet. Know that you must say no to yourself sometimes.

3. *Work on your discipline:* When it comes to anything productive in life, you are relying on your sense of discipline to guide you toward your goals. If you are given the choice between going to work and watching TV without any consequences for your actions, you'd likely choose TV. Try shifting this balance.

Select the option that allows you to have the most productivity. This is how you work on your self-discipline. The thing about it is that no one else is going to push you to get better at it — you are only relying on yourself.

4. Create a morning routine. The way that you start your day paves the path toward how the rest of your day is going to turn out. If you begin in a rushed and stressed state of being, then it is likely that you are going to feel on edge for the rest of the day.

Find a morning routine that works well for you and allows you to get everything done before you must leave your house. In order to make this easier, you might want to consider waking up earlier or showering at night so that you have a little bit of extra time to work with.

5. Pick your prime: Each person is going to have the time of day when they find that they operate best. For some, this is the first thing in the morning. Others prefer nighttime. No matter when this is for you, try to get a lot of your most challenging tasks done during this time if you can.

By working with your strengths, you are going to be making your life a lot easier. This step works especially great for tasks that don't necessarily have a strict deadline. When you can work on them at your own leisure, you will find a better end result if you work during your prime time.

Quick Start Action Step

This step is going to be very similar to the last one that you have just accomplished — you must schedule a time for when you are going to set your priorities. By taking a look at your tasks, you will notice that some of them jump out at you due to their deadlines or importance. These are the tasks that you must prioritize.

Remember, anything that can wait does not need to go on the priority list. While you do need to make sure that you also accomplish it, you can rest assured knowing that you will still be able to do this after you have taken care of the tasks that hold more importance.

Chapter 5:
New Habits, Better Routine

Chapter 5: New Habits, Better Routine

In this section, you will learn how to retrain yourself to live more productively. Any habits that are holding you back will be replaced with ones that better serve your routine and your life. The first step to taking control of your habits is your desire to strive for better ones.

Consider which qualities you wish you had. You can think about some people who inspire you for some ideas. Instead of simply wishing that you could be as productive as some of the people that you know, you will be able to transform your old habits into ones that allow you to make the most of your time.

1. Omit distractions.

When you are working on forming new habits, it is important to eliminate the distractions that are normally present in your work environment. Whether you are physically at work or simply taking care of chores at home, you need to make sure that you are able to stay on track.

Anything around you can serve as a distraction. Its ability to impact you depends on your level of concentration in that given moment. If you are truly focused, you will not give in to these things. In order to avoid giving in, it is best if you can place yourself in a quiet and calm environment where you are able to focus.

Social media and side conversations can be very entertaining. They can also be a way to brighten your day, but there is a time and a place for everything. Know that these activities are best done during your free time when you aren't presently working on goals.

2. Banish multitasking.

It is important that you are always one step ahead of the next thing you must do, but this does not necessarily mean that you have to break your concentration. Multitasking is one of the most common ways that people tend to get off track.

When you multitask, the quality of your work is diminished. Because you are focusing on more than one end result at one time, you have a higher likelihood of spreading yourself thin. This is a horrible feeling that leaves you wishing you had more time in a day.

Multitasking is also another way for you to unknowingly distract yourself. When there is too much stimulation, your brain tends to jump from topic to topic. This is the feeling that you get when you cannot seem to focus on what is right in front of you.

3. Don't overwork yourself.

Thinking about your physical and mental health, you are not going to be able to complete any task without either one of them. You are only human, so you are only going to be able to comprehend so much information. Try to be compassionate with yourself.

Pushing yourself is great; it allows you to break barriers and see how much more productive you can be. It becomes a counterproductive action, however, when you are suffering because of it. When you get things done, you should feel great. A feeling of stress indicates that you are overworking yourself.

Check yourself regularly to make sure that you are doing okay. Stop for breaks if you need to, and move things around on your schedule in a way that correctly aligns with your priorities. When you are flexible to changes, you will find it easy to do these things in order to preserve your health.

Steps to Take

Forming new habits does not need to be a drastic change that happens immediately. As you have learned, turning your goals into step-by-step tasks allows you to feel that you have more control over a situation. Consider the following steps when you are creating new habits to live your life by:

1. Make a commitment to change your behavior for 30 days.
2. Enforce your new habits daily, replacing your old ones as necessary.
3. Start with simple steps that can evolve into more complex ones.
4. Remind yourself about your new habits regularly.
5. Tell people that you trust about what you are doing.
6. Allow space for any imperfections that begin to surface.
7. Jump back on the bandwagon if you fall off.
8. Commit to another 30 days once you have

completed your first month.

By committing to a certain time period, you are giving yourself a definitive window of time in which you plan on actively trying to make your life better. While it can be easy to say that you are going to do this all the time and that you will start immediately, most people do not.

With all of the things that life brings your way, it becomes too easy to get sucked into your routine that you are familiar with. From the way that you work to the way that you interact with your loved ones, you can alter these habits in order to better serve your lifestyle of excellent time management.

While using the focus that you have been perfecting, implement your new habits into your life. Do not worry about easing into these things or doing them halfway. It is best to just begin doing them and to let the rest of your life adjust to this change.

If you get used to only doing something halfway, this causes a rift in your time management skills. You might begin to rely on this unfinished method too much, therefore putting you into a situation that was as minimally productive as the one you were in previously. Again, these habits do not need to be complex to start out. Even something as simple as making sure that you wake up 10 minutes earlier each workday can make a huge difference.

Though it might seem pointless at the moment, be sure to set regular reminders for yourself about your new way of life. Since these habits aren't going to be habits for you and your life just yet, you will need to make sure that you stay on track somehow. A simple reminder about the change that you are aiming for can be enough to kick your motivation into gear.

When you are able to stay motivated, you know that excellent results are going to follow. Take this as a personal challenge to change your routine for the better. While developing these new habits, you are on your way to a more efficient and successful way of taking action.

When you tell people what you are doing, this is not for bragging rights, although it is perfectly fine to feel proud of yourself for embarking on this journey. Telling those who care about you that you are aiming for a healthier way of living is going to boost your motivation even more. Because of the close bond that you share with these people, they are likely going to display positive reactions regarding your decision.

You will probably be able to find support within this group of people that you tell. While this step is completely optional, it does make a difference when you are able to talk to someone about your struggles and your triumphs with sticking to your new habits.

You are going to encounter some setbacks; that's okay! Your old habits are rooted deeply in the way that you operate, so it is likely that you are going to forget about your new ones or simply revert to your old ways. Punishing yourself isn't going to help you keep moving forward.

While it is natural to feel disappointed in yourself when you cannot abide by your new habits, there is always something that can be done in order to enforce them better. Instead of sulking and thinking about the things that you cannot do, think about all the things that you can do. What allows you to reach this point? Think about the various ways that you draw in strength to get things done.

If you notice that you are struggling a lot with remembering your new habits, then you should be able to see the areas in which you are weaker. Again, instead of punishing yourself for this, turn your weakness into a strength. For example, if you eat food late at night, try to make sure that you do not eat in bed. Eating in bed is only going to promote your bad habit and make it easily accessible for you to eat late into the night.

Simple fixes like this can do wonders for you if you are struggling with your new habits. You might need to try several different methods in order to find which ones you respond best to.

Quick Start Action Step

Take a moment to sit down and think about all of the new habits you would like to take on. Envision yourself becoming great at these habits, and think about all of the benefits that they would bring into your life. Now, think about ways that you can implement these behaviors into your daily life.

When they become so regular, you automatically become used to them. The behaviors that were once a challenge to remember will now be second nature to you. Make sure that you follow through with the above steps and tips regarding forming new habits.

Chapter 6:
How to Overcome Procrastination

Chapter 6: How to Overcome Procrastination

Procrastination is your body's natural way of protecting you against stress. If you feel overwhelmed by a task, it is likely that you might procrastinate in order to manage the way that you are feeling. This is how procrastination can become a problem that is so hard to solve. Since stress is a natural part of life, it is almost impossible to avoid it.

How can you ensure that you are properly managing your stress and not relying on procrastination? When you feel that you need to put something off until later, ask yourself if there is a deadline. Anything that has a deadline should not be procrastinated, whether it is due in one week or one hour.

When your body is faced with this kind of a threat, the procrastination comes in to prevent you from experiencing it. Mentally, you feel like you are doing yourself a favor, but in reality, you are actually making your future schedule even harder to manage than it was originally.

Why Procrastination Exists

1. *Emotional responsiveness:* Remember that procrastination is deeply rooted in your emotions. Whenever you are feeling overwhelmed or stressed out, it is likely that the thought of procrastinating comes to mind. This provides you with a way to regulate your emotions.

2. *Short-term relief:* Procrastination is simply a way to provide yourself with instant gratification. If you are feeling bad, then taking a break will allow you to free yourself from the negativity. While this sounds great in theory, it is only pushing the feeling aside for it to return again soon.

3. *Separation of self:* It is thought that we see ourselves as two separate people — our present selves and our future selves. This explains a lot of the reasoning behind why we feel that it is okay to procrastinate because we cannot exactly apply the repercussions that we will face in the future to our present selves.

4. *Priority on comfort:* Above all, humans crave

comfort. You would likely rather procrastinate your tasks in order to feel that you are in control of your life instead of experiencing temporary discomfort. This becomes apparent in the way that it is so easy to give in to the feeling that procrastination provides.

Steps to Take

One of the hardest habits to overcome, procrastination affects millions of people each day. You don't even need to be at work in order to feel the impacts of procrastination. It can happen at any time, anywhere. If you aren't careful, it is likely to become a regular part of your daily routine.

When you reach a point that you realize procrastination is holding you back from using your time efficiently, there are several ways that you can work on breaking the habit. From providing yourself with replacement behaviors to remembering the total impact of procrastination, you should be able to see things clearer.

Any task that you take on, no matter how stressful, can be managed in a way that is healthy to both your present self and your future self. There is no reason that you should have to suffer because of this. Awareness is going to make the process of ending procrastination a lot easier for you.

Allow these steps to guide you through various ways that you can eliminate procrastination from your routine:

1. *Take away the discomfort.* It is known that discomfort leads to procrastination, so it makes sense to try to combat the behavior from the source. Remind yourself that nothing is worth risking your physical and mental health over. Give yourself extra time to accomplish the task or try a new method, anything to help ease the stress.

2. *Remind your present self that your future self exists.* While it can be hard to remember this at the moment, it is a very real issue that you must face. Anything that you do to yourself or for yourself right now is going to affect the way that you feel later on. While things might seem like they have minimal consequences currently, you are going to feel them later.

3. *Set easy goals in the beginning.* Much like

setting attainable time management goals is a great way to start improving those skills, you can apply the same concept to beating procrastination. You don't need to give yourself too many tasks at once. Stick to the basics, and allow yourself some easy ones at first.

4. Learn how to ask for help. Procrastination often happens because you feel that you do not have enough time to accomplish a task. Whether you are at work or around the house, asking for help is a viable option that can ease your struggle. You will never know how much it can help unless you try to ask someone.

5. Think about the bigger picture. While you are overwhelmed right now, consider the end result of the goal that you are trying to accomplish. Know that the feeling isn't going to last forever, and soon you will be able to enjoy the hard work that you have put into the task. All tasks that are put off for later must be returned to in the near future.

6. Train yourself to finish tasks ahead of schedule. Instead of leaving important tasks to be done at the last minute, place them on your schedule in a way that suggests you have a little less time. Not only does this create a buffer for you, but it also encourages you to work proactively. When you get into this habit, you will be working more efficiently.

7. Redirect your tasks as necessary. If you have three tasks to complete that must all be done by the end of the day, it doesn't really matter what order you do them in. When you experience a task that is causing you trouble, you can choose a few options: stop working on it to breathe, work on a task that is easier, or work on a task that is harder.

8. Forgive your mistakes because they are bound to happen. When you procrastinate, the one who suffers the most is you. Keep this in mind the next time that you choose procrastination over productivity. While this is known, also keep in mind that you do need to forgive yourself if procrastination happens. Know that you are trying your best.

Become familiar with these steps and utilize them often. When you are able to work with the time that you have and the tasks that you have, there is simply no room for procrastination. It only exists in a space where you believe that you have more time than you do.

While you might be making the time for procrastination, it is ultimately not going to serve you well in the end. You will actually realize that you could've just made the time to work on your task instead of putting it off and facing double the effort now.

It is all a part of a learning experience. Some people are naturally more inclined to procrastination than others, and that is okay. Know where you stand on the topic, and make sure that your actions line up with your words. While you do not have to prove yourself to others, it becomes a nice challenge to prove to yourself that you can cut the procrastination from your life.

Quick Start Action Step

The next time that you feel like you could put something off for later, ask yourself what triggered this response. Are you overwhelmed or stressed out? Are you simply bored at the idea of completing the task? Deep down, there is a reason why you want to put it off.

Now, imagine the future impacts of your decision to procrastinate on this task. You are still going to have to get it done. Putting it off does not mean that it is going to disappear entirely. You are also going to have to work harder if there is a deadline involved.

It makes the most sense to encourage yourself to act now! Think about the instant gratification that you will get from accomplishing this task immediately. Imagine how great you will feel about yourself when you can go home and relax without having to worry about other tasks that are still on your mind. This is an ideal way to live your life stress-free and under control.

Consider breaking your task down into smaller steps if it feels too overwhelming to complete. Remember how much more attainable your goals seem when they are broken down instead of taken on whole? Do your best to map out a plan that is going to lead you to success.

When you become great at figuring out where your procrastination stems from, you will know what tools you need in order to succeed. Sometimes, laziness requires us to need a push of inspiration from other people. Other times, stress can cause us to need a sanctuary. Listen to what your mind and body are telling you.

Chapter 7: Starting the Day Right

Chapter 7: Starting the Day Right

While you've heard that breakfast is the most important meal of the day, did you also know that your morning routine has a lot to do with your continued success throughout the day? The way that you start your day has the ability to impact your mood and behavior greatly. When you are feeling great, your actions reflect this. A poor mood can lead to bad habits.

In theory, if you are able to get through your morning like a champ, then this means that the rest of your day should go just as smoothly. The way that you first handle things after you wake up says a lot about who you are as a person. Some of us are naturally inclined to work in the morning, while others would rather save this productivity for later on in the day.

To become the most successful person that you can be, you must try to harness all of your most productive energy into your mornings. From the way that you treat yourself as you wake up to the way that you enter your place of work, you need to be aware of how you are feeling.

Things can happen to you while you are getting ready that have the ability to mess up your entire day, but it is up to you to not let that happen. You are in total control of your own day. While you cannot direct what others do, you can be responsible for your own actions and ideas. Present other people with the same energy that you would like in return.

An Early Start

Waking up earlier is your secret to getting a better start to your day. While the idea might not sound appealing to you, it is important to think about all of the ways in which this will benefit you. A lot of wasted time happens when you stay up too late and are then forced to rush in the morning.

When you regulate your sleep schedule, you are giving yourself more time to do the things that are necessary to keep your day running smoothly. If you are constantly rushing to get to work on time or to drop the kids off at school, you are going to be more likely to forget things.

Having a clear and recharged mind is going to help you effectively get through every task that you must complete. These are a few of the benefits that you will notice by getting a better start to your day:

1. A stress-free start

Instead of waking up and feeling that you have a million things to do, you will be able to feel at ease. When you leave tasks for yourself to do the following day, they have the ability to build up. Because of this, you might worry about them through the night, preventing yourself from getting adequate rest.

Try to do something relaxing to ease yourself into the morning when you first wake up. This can be anything from enjoying a cup of tea to taking a hot shower. Make sure that the first thing you do does not involve a screen of any kind. This is to ensure that your mind stays relaxed until you are fully awake.

As you begin getting ready, try to only focus on that task. If you start your day with multitasking, then you are likely to continue multitasking throughout the day. It can become a bad habit if you are not careful.

Get yourself ready and get the kids ready if you need

to. Focus on each task as a whole — getting dressed, making breakfast, and packing bags. When you are able to stay focused, the process becomes a lot faster.

2. *The habit of a routine*

As it was discussed in the previous chapter, creating better habits for yourself makes it more possible to keep a routine of productivity. If you start to wake up just 10 minutes earlier each day, you are solidifying this as a new habit in your life. You can keep working in increments until you are waking up as early as you would like.

Your morning routine is going to be the backbone of your day. What you are able to accomplish in the morning will motivate you to do more as you get through your day. Do not forget to include a healthy breakfast in your routine. Along with sleep, food is going to give you additional energy that is essential to the way that you will function.

Keeping yourself in a great mood is also going to make a difference in your morning routine. This is why it is not the best idea to start off your morning by looking at screens. Anything that is going on in the news or on social media has the ability to change the way that you feel, sometimes in negative ways. Try to surround yourself with positivity at all times.

3. A head start on time management

The way that you use your time when you first wake up sets the standard for how you are going to use the rest of your time. If you procrastinate or put things off, you know that this is just going to add more tasks to your schedule during the day.

Getting out the door is one of the very first tasks that anyone accomplishes. It is one that is very important. If you are able to successfully walk out the door with a few minutes to spare, then you are on the right track. Whenever you feel rushed, you will know that something in your morning routine must change.

You might need to do more preparation for your day at night before you go to sleep, or you might need to wake up a little bit earlier in order to make sure that everything gets done. The goal is to get to a point where you feel comfortable and confident as you walk out the door.

If you are able to accomplish this, your time management skills will continue to develop as you need them throughout the day. Anything that happens at work is going to be taken care of with the same clear mind and productive spirit. This is what you must strive for.

Steps to Take

In order to wake up earlier, the easiest way to begin is by starting right away. If you put it off, you are only going to begin to dread the idea. This doesn't have to be a negative or bothersome task. The sooner that you do it, the sooner your body will regulate itself. By following these steps, you will feel great about your new morning routine and starting your day off right:

1. Prepare the night before.

No matter what you need to do, try to get as much as you can done before you go to sleep. This includes things like bathing the children, packing school lunches, and setting out clothes that you plan on wearing.

Small steps like these will save you time in the morning. It might seem like an insignificant amount, but it could make a difference between walking out the door late or early. Any time that you can save is also going to mean that you can sleep in a little longer.

2. Relax before you fall asleep.

It can be tempting to catch up on all that you have missed throughout the day, but overstimulation is one of the main things that will keep you awake at night. While it is okay to look at these things after you have finished your tasks, make sure that you put an end to it as you unwind for the night.

Try to read or write as you get settled into bed. Any remaining ideas that you have in your mind should be let go of as you calm down. If you need more help to relax, try taking a nice lavender bath or drinking a cup of caffeine-free tea. This is going to help you let go of any stress that remains.

3. Don't snooze your alarm clock, not even once.

While snoozing gives you the illusion that you are getting more rest, it actually makes it harder for you to finally get out of bed. When your alarm goes off, you can get up at a reasonable speed.

Start by opening your eyes and stretching your body.

You can spend a few minutes doing this before you sit up fully. Make sure that you are going at a speed that is reasonable enough that you stay on track while also allowing your mind and body time to get moving.

As soon as you train your body to start the process of waking up as the alarm goes off, you are going to get used to it. People feel the need to snooze their alarm because they still feel tired. Your goal should be to get to a point where you actually feel rested at night, and the steps prior to this one will help you get there.

Quick Start Action Step

In order to prepare for a better night's sleep, eliminate your screen time an hour before you plan on going to bed. This is something that you can implement right away. Look to other activities that can help you unwind without stimulating your mind too much.

Be firm with yourself and your decision to get better rest. Think about the bigger picture and how you will use this extra time to make your life easier. You won't have to struggle to get your tasks done. Instead, you will have time to spare that you can use on fun things.

Chapter 8: Managing Time at Work

Chapter 8: Managing Time at Work

A lot of stress that you encounter on an average day comes from tasks that you do at work. While it can be easy enough to regulate your own schedule and your own routine, you don't always get this freedom in the workplace. Because there are people to answer to and deadlines to meet that you do not make, you must take extra care that you are not stressing yourself out to the point where you become stagnant.

Having a great professional relationship with those you work with is going to make your life easier. When you have open communication with your boss and your peers, you will have the ability to ask for help if you need it. This is something that you should not feel ashamed of doing.

We all need help sometimes, and it shows great time management skills when you have the ability to ask for it. Alternatively, your peers will also see that you are open to helping them. If you have this type of professional relationship, it is going to work out in everyone's favor.

Saying no is also an important thing to learn. It can be very difficult to simply say no to someone without a reason that you find "good enough." Know that it is your right to say no. If your coworker asks you for help yet you are behind on your own tasks, you should say no at this moment.

Taking on additional responsibilities while you are already behind in your own is a sure way to stress yourself out. This is exactly what you must avoid in order to have a healthy work environment. Remember that you should never feel as though you are spreading yourself too thin.

When you are managing your time better at work, you will be able to notice these differences right away:

1. Increased productivity: When your day moves along at the pace you select, your productivity is going to increase. You will feel motivated to get through each task with the promise of relaxation waiting for you at the end of each day.

2. Better mood: Your mood affects the people around you. Not only does it have the ability to add to your potentially bad day, but it can also cause others to have a bad day. The way that you treat people is going to impact the overall work environment. Time that is managed efficiently will keep you happy.

3. Excellent focus: By working on a single task at a time, you are going to be able to make the most of your effort. Instead of having to divide your concentration because you need to take on multiple tasks at once, you can ensure that you have enough time to get everything completed while staying on track.

Steps to Take

If you are currently struggling with the amount of time that you have while you are at work, these simple steps are going to help you realize that you have more time to work with than you originally thought. With better distribution and focus, you will see that it is possible to retrain yourself to make the most of the time that you have. These are the steps to follow in order to make the most of the time that you spend at work:

1. *Have breakfast.* While this step sounds trivial, it becomes the foundation for your time spent at work. Having enough energy is going to ensure that you have focus. Whether you need to eat at home as a part of your morning routine or eat at work to start your day, make sure that you are consuming something nutritious.

2. *Work by the deadline.* Your tasks should be prioritized by order of importance, so consider which ones need to be done immediately. It is always smart to start with these tasks at the beginning of your day so that you don't have to spend the end of your day rushing to complete them.

3. *Take breaks.* Giving yourself proper breaks can be just as important as making sure that you are completing your work. We all need some time to reset, especially after we have been working on something challenging or time-consuming. Taking a few moments to step out of your workspace to breathe will allow your brain to rest.

4. *Get rid of distractions.* Being on your phone while you work isn't going to make the process go by any faster. It actually might end up causing you delays. Whether you are getting distracted by screens or spending too much time talking to your peers, you must make sure that you are placing the most focus on your tasks at hand.

5. *Have a sense of humor.* Being too serious while you work can potentially lead you to a bad mood or tension with your peers. It is important that you still know how to laugh about things even when everything is going wrong. Taking yourself too seriously at work is one way to become easily stressed out. Do your best to find humor in all that you do.

6. *Get organized before you go home.* It might be your first instinct to run out the door as soon as work is over, but you must make sure that you are preparing your future self for the day ahead. If you have anything that you can sort through and organize that will make your life easier, do so before you leave. You will thank yourself for this step, as it will make your next day run smoothly.

7. *Ask for help on pending tasks.* As you approach the end of each day, you should have a basic idea of how much additional time you are going to need in order to finish tasks that are incomplete. This is when you should consider asking for help or deadline extensions, if possible. Do not wait until the last minute as you are struggling to meet deadlines.

8. *Stay optimistic.* No matter how bad or good your day was, know that the feeling is only temporary. Allow yourself to be proud of what you have accomplished, yet do not get caught up on the things that you wish you could have done. Tomorrow brings another chance for you to regroup your thoughts and ideas so that you can try again.

9. *Keep work at work.* When you leave your job, make sure that you leave any stress there too. It can become a problem if you are taking these feelings home with you after your day has already ended. You might be unintentionally taking out your negativity on your spouse or children when you do this. It can also disrupt your sleep schedule, causing you to feel bad when you wake up the next morning.

10. *Celebrate all victories.* No matter if you completed a hundred tasks or one task in a day, it is rightful for you to be proud of yourself for getting through it. Despite all of the things that could work against you, recognize that you are doing your best and making the most out of the time you have. Some days are going to be better than others, but you can always feel proud of what you have accomplished.

Quick Start Action Step

At the end of your next workday, ensure that you have organized all of your future work in a way that will allow things to run smoothly. Do not leave anything incomplete without a plan about how you are going to get it done as soon as possible. As you leave, make sure that you remember all you accomplished that day and allow yourself to be proud of these accomplishments.

Leaving work in a good mood is a great way to set yourself up for a productive day tomorrow. No matter what you had to go through, know that you are going to come back the next day with a refreshed outlook and ample motivation. The moment that you step out the door, know that there is no use holding on to any stress or worry that is attached to your job.

You will work on these things again the following day with your plan in place. There is no use stressing about things at home, where nothing can actually be done. This signifies the time when you must put work aside in order to focus on the next tasks at hand.

Chapter 9: Managing Time at Home

Chapter 9: Managing Time at Home

All of your time spent at home must be divided between various things. From spending time with your loved ones to completing chores, this time is actually some of your most diverse. While you might be great at managing your time at work, do not forget to manage it when you are at home as well.

Having structure, even for the things that you enjoy, is how you are going to make sure that you do everything you want to do. A healthy balance between your work life and personal life is going to make you the happiest. If one is neglected, you will be faced with the feeling to overcompensate.

Your schedule is very important for making sure that you are doing all that you need to do while being at home. From tasks to activities, it is important that you are including everything on your schedule. Staying organized will allow you to see the bigger picture of what is in store for you.

Commit to the things that you want to do even if they

are leisure activities. For example, if you promised the kids a trip to the park, put that on the schedule. This small bit of time is going to allow you to bond with your children while doing something fun. It is right of you to include that into your list of priorities even if it doesn't revolve around doing chores.

For the tasks that are more like work, try to get these done during one of your peak times if possible. This is a time when you are able to function at your best. If this doesn't work for your schedule, you can try to spread your chores out over the entire day. Also, don't forget that you can utilize the help of other household members.

Achieving this balance is not difficult, and you will feel more at ease as soon as you are able to find the balance. Allow yourself to enjoy these benefits as you become better at managing your time at home:

1. Expert planning

When you are at home, you are likely responsible for more than just your own activities. From things that the kids would like to do to things that matter to your spouse, being able to plan for them all is going to help you accomplish a balance in your life.

Planning allows you to stay ahead. You will be able to prepare in all ways necessary before you begin each activity. Remember, even the things that you do in your free time might require some preparation. Having this time to prepare, no matter what you are doing, is going to keep your schedule on track.

2. Clean living space

When you stay on top of your chores, you stay on top of the things that must be cleaned. Cleaning up around the house can be a bothersome task when you feel that you are short on time, but when you are planning for it, this should be fairly easy to accomplish.

If you make sure to do some cleaning each day, then you will avoid having to do a lot all at once. This is a tip for keeping your chores manageable. Know that you do not have to do it alone too. Your household is responsible as a whole for the cleanliness of the home. Involve the entire family when it comes to chores!

3. Organized belongings

There is nothing worse than trying to leave your house yet being held up because you can't find something.

Staying organized is a way to avoid this problem, and it is something that you will begin to prioritize as you start better managing your time at home.

You should be able to know where everything is in case you need it. Spending minutes or even hours looking for something that you know is there can be insanely frustrating. This gets your stress level up, potentially even ruining your time spent at home. Incorporate organization into your regular chores to ensure that you know where your belongings are.

4. More enjoyment

When you are at home, you should feel a sense of relief. Your house should be your safe space, a sanctuary that you feel comfortable in. When it is too messy or you have too much to accomplish, you can begin to resent the feeling of being at home because it stresses you out.

As you start implementing your time management skills while you are at home, you will find that you enjoy doing things in your house a lot more. Being at home doesn't always have to revolve around doing chores. As long as you are making regular progress, you should no longer feel burdened to get everything done all at once.

Steps to Take

1. *Make sure that your schedule is set for the upcoming week.* Include all of your tasks and your activities on it. Take a look at everything that you must do, and make changes as necessary in order to balance your time. Are you leaving enough room for fun things?

2. *Relax during your time to relax.* Do not try to get a few quick chores done during your designated relaxation time. Your mind is never going to shut off if you are constantly worrying about doing the most that you can. Remember that relaxation is just as important as working. You need to be sure that you are focusing on it too.

3. *Spend guilt-free time with your family.* Much like your relaxation time, you must make sure that you aren't multitasking during family time. Being present is important for strengthening the bonds that you have. It also helps to relieve any stress that you might still be holding on to. Enjoy this time because you deserve it.

4. *Organize while you clean.* When you clean up around your house, you are going to be getting rid of the things that no longer serve a purpose. After you do this, you are going to be in a place where you can put everything away in an organized manner. These two separate tasks can actually be turned into one, saving you time.

5. *Stick to your sleep schedule.* Sleep is one of the first things that become compromised when you feel that you do not have time to finish the tasks you have around the house. Do not allow yourself to get less sleep just because you feel that you must make up for the lost time. Instead, fix the problem by getting up earlier.

As you can see, it does not take a lot for you to handle the time that you have at home. You likely already have an idea of what needs to be done and what you would like to do. The hardest part is fitting it all into one schedule. With the proper modifications, you can do this while not sacrificing anything in the process.

A common misconception is that we must give up our free time in order to work on chores. When you do this, you are only adding stress to your life; there comes a point when you will need relief. This is why ensuring that you plan for fun activities is so important. It is how you maintain a balance in your home life.

Quick Start Action Step

Survey your current schedule and compare the ratio of chores to fun activities. A step that you can take immediately is to ensure that you have a balance between the two. Add things to your schedule as necessary in order to achieve this. You can also modify your schedule by splitting up certain tasks so that you have additional time.

This step takes no time at all, yet it has the ability to make the time that you spend at home a lot more enjoyable. Remember, you are in control over your own schedule at home. Use this flexibility to your advantage by making plans that make sense with the time that you have.

Inform all of the other household members of your schedule and future plans. You might find that you are able to collaborate on some of these tasks, further eliminating your workload. It is a good idea to keep the schedule in a place that is visible to all family members. Encourage them to give you some suggestions on things that they would like to fit on the schedule.

Chapter 10:
Tools and Apps to Help You

Chapter 10: Tools and Apps to Help You

While you have probably considered all of the ways in which technology can hinder your time management skills, there are also plenty of ways that it can help you. Organization apps are a great tool to utilize when you are looking to turn your lost time into time that could be spent on productivity. No matter what kind of device you have, there is a way to incorporate an app into your daily routine that can help you.

There are apps that go beyond providing you with a calendar to refer to. From digital grocery lists to apps that help you budget your expenses, there are so many ways that you can use technology to help you save time. The best part is, a lot of these apps will not cost you any money. Most of them are available for free on their given platform.

Benefits of Using Apps

1. No physical space: Using your phone, computer, or tablet to store this type of information is great for clutter purposes. While you can write down lists and make charts, this can often backfire because it requires you to physically create each item. Digital apps make the process a lot more simple and streamlined.

2. *Always with you:* If you have ever written down a list, there is a chance that you have forgotten it when you need it most. By having your information on your device, you are much more likely to have it with you always. There is no need to remember to take anything additional with you no matter where you need to go.

3. *Easy to share:* If you need to share any type of list or schedule, you won't have to make additional copies of it when you are utilizing an app. With the click of a button, nearly all of the apps that you can download to help you with productivity are shareable with other users. Your whole household can be following the same schedule with the same ability to add things to it.

4. *Science-backed technology:* A lot of apps that are available for you include extensive research behind them. Not only can you feel great about the efficiency of the app that you choose, but you can also have confidence in its ability to help you. Many apps have the ability to assess the way that you think, therefore being able to motivate you individually.

5. *Ease of access:* There is nothing more frustrating than not being able to find what you are looking for during an important moment. You will never lose your schedule when it is being stored in a productivity app. If you ever need to quickly reference something, you will be able to do so in no time at all.

6. *Ability to set aside:* When your tasks are located within an app, you will be less tempted to look at them and worry about them during your free time. Remember, your free time is just as important as your time spent working. Designate a time when you are supposed to be looking at the productivity apps and make sure that you adhere to this time.

7. *Extra motivation:* Even if the app that you use isn't meant to be motivational, seeing everything in front of you is a way to inspire you. There is a unique feeling that you get from taking a look at a full schedule, and you have the ability to either work toward accomplishing it or let it overwhelm you. As you work with apps more, you will learn how to view this as something that is helpful.

8. Back-up features: If you have ever written down something important and lost it, you know how devastating this can feel. Losing valuable information is a big setback that would normally cost you additional time. Since most of these apps have a back-up feature, you never have to worry about personally keeping track of your information. Even if your device is compromised, the back-up should extend to a source that is accessible from other devices.

9. Privacy and security: With the help of a password-protected device, your information is automatically going to be much more secure than it would be if you utilize physical methods of keeping a schedule. Instead of worrying about other people reading your tasks or finding your to-do lists, you can rest assured knowing that only you have access to this information because only you have access to your device.

Steps to Take

The following are some of the most helpful apps to download:

1. *Rescue Time:* This is an app that runs in the background on your phone to track how much time is spent on each task that you perform in a day. Once you input the times, you will get a detailed report at the end of each day with a breakdown of how you managed your time.

2. *Pocket:* If you have ever come across something online that you'd like to click on but you're busy working on a separate task, this app will store it in a "pocket" so that you can return to it when you have free time.

3. *Focus@Will:* Meant to incorporate neuroscience and music, this app helps your brain get back into a focused state. You can use it when you are in need of a boost in productivity.

4. *Mind42:* Utilizing mind mapping, you can use this app to see exactly what you need to focus on based on your tasks at hand. You are able to create to-do lists, brainstorm, and even share your map with other users.

5. Remember the Milk: Much more than a grocery list app, you can use this one to list your tasks, when they are due, and who is responsible for them. Compatible with many devices, you will never miss a task. It has an easy-to-use and straightforward interface that many users enjoy.

6. Evernote: This is a productivity app that has been around for years. Mainly used by college students in the past, it allows you to collect and store ideas. You can create notes, add attachments, utilize voice memos, and more using this app.

7. Dropbox: Mainly used as a platform where you can share large files easily, it is a very simple app to use. Given its recent popularity, it is also one that has less of a learning curve because so many people are already familiar with it.

8. MyLifeOrganized: This app does exactly what it sounds like it would. By giving you custom made to-do lists, you will be able to get to work immediately. It even highlights the tasks that you should be prioritizing. You are also able to access a chart that shows your progress and a list of objectives to ensure you stay on track.

9. *Calendar:* Any mobile device will come equipped with some type of calendar feature. Use this tool often as it is a way for you to always stay up to speed with all of the things that you need to do. Get into the habit of adding your tasks to your digital calendar and sync it to all of your devices if possible.

10. *Timer:* Another feature that comes with mobile devices is the timer — this can help you more than you realize. When you are working on many different tasks that require you to divide your time, use a timer to make sure that time is being distributed as it should be.

Quick Start Action Step

Review the list of apps and tools above and select one to download today. Select the one that you feel is going to benefit you most and help make your life more efficient. Once you have it, make sure that you set it up fully, adding all of the necessary details that the app requires. Waiting to add these details later is only going to promote procrastination.

Make sure that you get into the habit of using the app

every day, as it should become a part of your daily routine. During some free time, make sure that you become familiar with it and explore all of the features that it has to offer. Make a commitment that you are going to use it consistently for at least 30 days.

If it doesn't already track your progress, make sure to keep your own record of how much better you become with time management. Since the app is going to be on your mobile device, there will be no excuses for not using it. Digital apps change the way that you are able to enhance your productivity. Once you form the habit, you will see how much these apps can help you by encouraging you to stay focused and be efficient.

Chapter 11: Dealing with Distractions

Chapter 11: Dealing with Distractions

The life of a busy woman is not exclusive to her own problems and tasks — it can extend to the problems and tasks of others, as well. If you utilize any form of social media, you know how easy it can be to stay on the app for much longer than anticipated. Social media is like a gateway to information in abundance. Since everyone has the freedom to share what they want, you could easily spend hours on a platform, getting lost in the commotion.

If you have ever had a hard time focusing on your priorities, these apps are likely to blame. While they are not the only distractions that exist, they are among the most persistent. We often like to check them because they are ever-changing. Depending on how many people you friend/like/follow, you will receive new information to browse regularly.

It is like having a constant stream of your loved ones' lives on display at your fingertips. While there is nothing wrong with participating in social media yourself, you must ensure that you are doing so when the time is right. If you have tasks to do, getting on social media beforehand is never a good idea. Much like anything that is pending, you have the ability to become distracted, which can then lead to procrastination.

Why It Is Important

1. Being present: No matter what you are doing, it is essential that you are present in the given situation. If you are working while simultaneously browsing through social media, your attention isn't going to be in the right place. You might be able to get things done, but it is likely going to be of compromised quality and in more time.

2. Mental stimulation: It is thought that stimulating your brain with information is a great thing, but not when you are reading things that are only meant to distract or entertain you. Learning new information that can help you in life is different from browsing through social media. Keep this in mind when you feel that your brain is being stimulated by what you are reading.

3. Lack of sleep: A lot of people utilize distractions on their phones in order to help them sleep at night. While you might eventually feel tired, reading this type of information is actually going to be more likely to keep you awake. It is not a relaxing activity, but instead, one that can be overly stimulating. When you spend a lot of time reading about other people's problems and drama, you might also feel that you have to take on the same negative energy.

4. A rarity: When you begin to utilize social media only during times when you aren't in the middle of tasks, you will appreciate it for its entertainment purposes. It can become very easy to make browsing social media a habit that just turns into something that you *have* to do without even really knowing why. Use it only when you really feel like using it instead of as a form of distraction.

Steps to Take

Remember that getting rid of distractions does not equate to getting rid of fun. It is simply what you must learn how to do in order to stay focused when it matters. Social media is a way to free your mind and become unfocused. As long as you remember their individual purposes, then you should be on the right path toward creating more of a balance in your life.

Using these steps, ensure that you are making your life as distraction-free as you can:

1. Put your phone aside.

As long as you aren't working on your phone, there is no reason for you to be on it. Even a single glance at your screen can be enough to shift your focus. Make sure that you are truly considering your priorities, and get yourself used to the idea that your phone can be put away while you work.

A lot of people have become so dependent on their phones given the recent advancements in technology; this is natural. Phones can help you with organization while also keeping you connected to the people you care about. It makes sense that you would want to gravitate toward it at all times. It is also very easily accessible.

Work on keeping track of exactly when you feel like reaching for your phone. If it is a designated time to focus on work, then you do not need to be opening your social media apps for a "quick" look. Remember, what starts off as quick is often never going to be quick when it comes to these distractions.

2. *Make sure that background noise is kept to a minimum if you can help it.*

While you cannot always control your working environment, you can have preferences. Noise that is happening in the background might not seem like it affects you, but chances are that it does. Even if you stop for a moment to consider what noises you are hearing, this has the ability to alter your focus.

Listening to music while you are performing certain tasks can be relaxing, but it can also be very distracting. When your brain is forced to focus on two very distinct things, the quality of your work will become compromised. If you can help it, save the music for when you are finished with your tasks.

Everyone is different in their ability to function in hectic environments, but when you can help it, try to make it as peaceful as you can. This ensures that you are maintaining the right level of clarity to your thinking. Just because you can do something doesn't mean that you should.

3. Take breaks during your tasks.

As mentioned before, taking breaks is very important to your continued success. Sometimes, you can set yourself up with all of the necessary tools and the perfect environment, yet you will still end up becoming distracted. This could be an indication that you are overworking your brain. The easiest fix is to take a short break.

A break is literally meant to provide you with a stopping point before you are ready to fully stop what you are working on. Regrouping your thoughts can prove to be very beneficial when you are concentrating on a task. Ideas that you might be suppressing or that you might be forgetting have the ability to surface once you step away from said task.

Try taking short breaks the next time that you feel too overwhelmed and stressed out to continue your task. You will probably find that you are also less distracted when you practice this method. Because you are giving your brain a chance to reset, it is less likely to crave a distraction in the first place.

4. Get distracting thoughts out before you begin working.

It is natural that you are going to have a lot on your mind sometimes. No matter how hard you try to focus, it can seem impossible when you are distracted by thoughts going on inside of your own head.

Journaling can be a great fix for this problem. A few minutes of freewriting has the ability to promote more focus in your life. Instead of wasting time on the things that you cannot currently change, you will be able to sort through them before you begin the tasks that require the most concentration.

Having a conversation with someone you trust can also be a good fix for something like this. Getting distracting information off your chest is always a better option than trying to suppress it and live with it. You'll find that it always rises to the surface no matter how hard you try to prevent it from happening.

Quick Start Action Step

Pick up your phone and look through every single app that you currently have downloaded onto it. Don't spend too much time on this step, but make sure that you create a mental note each time that you encounter an app or feature that takes up a lot of your time. Some phones will be able to show you usage, highlighting which apps you spend the most time on and when you use them.

Uninstall the apps that you no longer use. This will free up some space on your phone and give you a cleaner appearance from your home screen. For the apps that are pure time killers, organize them all into a folder together. Make a promise to yourself that these apps are to be used during your free time only. If necessary, make the folder secure by placing a lock or passcode on it.

Anything that distracts you has the ability to drain your time and energy. These apps are like sugar — use them sparingly. This does not mean that you need to uninstall any fun app or social media app that you have ever downloaded, but it does mean that you need to work on your self-discipline in order to succeed with your time management skills.

Chapter 12: The Art of Delegation

Chapter 12: The Art of Delegation

Delegation is a very useful skill to learn for time management purposes. It requires a bit of letting go if you'd like it to work out in your favor, though. Letting go of control can be very difficult for some of us, especially when we are used to getting things done in a certain way. What you must realize is that there are many paths that can lead to the same end result.

When you delegate tasks, you are making the most of the help that you have around you. It isn't a weakness or something to be ashamed of. It actually takes a lot of strength to admit that you could use some help. Delegation is the process of selecting the right person to help you, not merely passing off your work onto someone else.

In its most traditional sense, delegation refers to the way that you can get your peers to assist you with work-related tasks. However, delegation is not only limited to workplace interactions. You can delegate tasks at home to your spouse and your children when you feel that you need some extra help. The concept applies no matter what task you are doing.

Once a task has been delegated to someone else, this does not necessarily mean that you get to sit back and relax while others take on your role. It can actually free up your time in order for you to spend it by working on more pressing matters. Having a solid sense of prioritization is essential in order to make this work its best for you. If you know that your time would be better spent on a different task yet the original one still needs to be completed, then delegation is a responsible decision.

It can be hard to imagine how you would just ask someone to do your task for you. This is why trust is very important. If you are a hard worker who does not hesitate to help those around you, then this is going to send a positive message. If you tend to keep to yourself and refuse to take on any additional work, then you might find it hard to get someone who is willing to complete your delegated tasks.

Your demeanor and integrity are everything when it comes to building your reputation. As long as you are known for being honest and fair, then you shouldn't have too much trouble bringing up the concept of delegation to your peers. You might be surprised to see how much those around you respect you because of the energy that you put off.

Even at home, you need to be a team player. If you always rely on your spouse to clean up around the house, delegating yet another chore to them is not going to make them feel great. In a fair household, all family members contribute to the tasks and chores involved with living in the home. Remember that you are all supposed to be working together in order to make your living space the best that it can be.

Delegation can definitely be a team-building activity when used correctly. Once the task is completed, you can share the joy and relief with the person that helped you get there. As you help more people, you will find that others become more willing to help you in return. It all becomes a domino effect that works out for everyone's benefit.

How It Can Be Difficult

Depending on the type of personality that you have, delegating a task to someone else can be an intimidating process. While you need to present confidence in the way that you approach the subject, you also need to believe in yourself enough to know that you deserve this help that you are asking for. It takes a little bit of practice in order to become comfortable with asking others for help. These are some of the most common struggles that you will run into when you are delegating tasks:

1. *Thinking you can do it better:* While you might have a very particular way of working, you aren't going to be able to free up your time until you let go of this control. Micromanaging people isn't a way to earn their trust; you must let go and let the results speak for themselves. Anyone who is qualified to do your tasks while also maintaining a great reputation is likely to meet your needs without much complication.

2. *Feeling intimidated by asking:* Selecting someone to delegate a task to is normally the easy part. The hard part happens when you must ask this person if they are willing to take on the task that you are delegating. If you are in a role where you are qualified to delegate tasks, then there is no need to feel intimidated. Think about the situation as a partnership rather than a supervisor/lower-level dynamic. You are still going to be on the same level because you both need to get this task done.

3. *Holding onto worry:* It becomes a problem if you continue to worry about a task that you have already delegated. The point of passing it along is to free up your time and clear your mind. You must learn how to let go of these things if you would like to be able to shift your focus onto something else. Know that the task is still in good hands.

Steps to Take

1. *Choose to delegate a task when it becomes too much for you to handle.* This will encourage you to delegate only when absolutely necessary. If you overdo it, your peers are going to feel taken advantage of.

2. *Select a person whom you feel is qualified.* Based on the task at hand and the work involved, think about whom you can trust to get this done. Who is closest to you in terms of skills and traits? You will want to pick someone whose values you agree with.

3. *Have a conversation with this person.* Make sure that all of the terms are clear to avoid any misunderstandings. You will want to explain why you are delegating the task, what it entails, and when it should be completed.

4. *Remain present in the background.* While you do not need to take this step literally, know that it is a kind thing to be there to answer questions in case the person has any. You are going to have the most knowledge about this task, so be helpful when you can.

5. *Check on progress without being overbearing.* Remember, you have delegated this task in order to free up your time. It should no longer be a priority to you because you should already be focusing on something else. Allow yourself to check with this person to keep the communication open, but do not try to micromanage.

These steps are simple, but they are designed to keep you on track with how and when you are delegating. As stated, the more that you get used to it, the easier it becomes. You will be able to use your best judgment in order to assess your workload and better maintain your schedule.

As people realize how dependable you are in return, they might ask you for the same favor. Help out when you can in order to keep things running smoothly. When people help one another, this promotes a healthy working environment.

Quick Start Action Step

Think about a recurring task that appears on your schedule. This task should be one that isn't particularly hard to accomplish yet easy for you to let go of. An example would be checking the mail. If you check the mail every single day, select this as your first task to delegate to someone else.

It is a small step, but it is how you are going to learn to delegate larger tasks. Practice your steps by acting confidently and kindly. If it goes well, you might be ready to move onto bigger things. Take note of any areas that feel intimidating or awkward. Work on how you can improve the way that you delegate tasks.

The frequency that you delegate and the way that you

do it is all up to your discretion. This is one of the best parts about delegation. While it feels that you must let go of all control, you do still have a great deal of it.

Chapter 13:
Finding Your Me Time

Chapter 13: Finding Your Me Time

When was the last time that you did something for yourself that you truly wanted to do? Playing with the kids, cooking for your spouse, and listening to friends talk are all wonderful and fulfilling activities on their own; but they serve a social purpose. The idea of me time to do something that you want to do that only benefits you.

The concept sounds selfish, but it is actually a very helpful addition to any working woman's schedule. First, know that you deserve me time. With all of the tasks that you take on each day, it is your right to take some time that is spent only on yourself. This does not need to be an excessive amount of time because you likely don't have much to spare, but it should be sufficient.

Think about the things that make you feel good, what you truly enjoy. This is going to be different for each woman because everyone has different interests. Me time is a sacred time that often gets pushed aside to make room for other things. Beginning now, you must make it a goal to prioritize me time each day.

Even if you are just sitting down with a book to read for 10 minutes, this still counts as me time if it is exactly what you'd like to be doing. Me time is ideally supposed to feel rejuvenating and calming. It is a way for you to get to know yourself and to check the way you're feeling.

You'd be surprised what you can learn from simply listening to the way you feel and the thoughts you have. If you notice that there is lingering unhappiness yet you are fulfilled in so many ways, you might be lacking me time in your schedule. It is a small addition that can make a huge difference.

Benefits of Me Time

If you still aren't convinced that you deserve this small bit of time to yourself, consider the benefits that you will feel. When you are committed to utilizing this time, you are placing a sense of greater value on your well-being. Instead of feeling like you have spent all your energy on other people, me time is a way for you to reserve some for yourself.

1. *Reduced stress:* As you know, stress is a common occurrence for most. The average person likely feels stressed out more than once per day. A lot of what induces stress comes from the expectations of others. Me time allows you to retreat and step away from the commotion that stress brings. By doing so, you are allowing your mind and body to recover while reducing your stress levels.

2. Self-discovery: Learning new things about yourself is important. You might feel that this is impossible as a grown adult, but you are a multi-faceted human being. As you grow and experience new things in life, you develop new traits. It is important to stay truly tapped into who you are as a person.

3. *Relationship Improvement:* Spending time alone actually helps the functionality of your relationships. As the popular saying suggests, absence does make the heart grow fonder. Even if you are only away from your loved ones for 10–15 minutes at a time, this space is healthy. You might even feel that you miss each other's company.

4. *Better balance:* You know how easy it can be to

incorporate work and chores onto your already-packed schedule. The hard part comes when you must balance it out by adding fun and exciting things onto it. Me time qualifies as one of the activities that will balance out your work. It allows you to let go of anything that you might still be holding onto.

5. *More concentration:* It can be hard to focus when there is too much going on around you. Stepping away from this type of environment to have me time can help you get your focus back when you return. Me time should be a welcomed change of scenery that you can rely on to bring you into a better mood.

Steps to Take

You might be convinced that you need more me time on your schedule, but how do you make this happen? It sounds too good to be true, but it doesn't have to be. By utilizing these simple steps, you can find some time to spend with yourself in order to ensure that you are the best version of yourself.

1. *Walk around.*

No matter where you are, a change in scenery is going to be a great way that you can spend some time with yourself. Whether you would like to take a walk around the block or simply walking down the hallway, you can spend some time with yourself while you clear your head.

This is a great first step toward incorporating more me time into your schedule because it doesn't change much at all. This isn't something that you need to rearrange tasks for. It is a way for you to have a break from whatever you are currently experiencing.

2. Listen to music.

Your favorite music has the ability to transport you to another place. It can calm you down, lift you up, and make you feel excited all at once. Allow yourself the joy of listening to some of your favorite music the next time that you require some alone time.

This is a great activity to incorporate into your me time because it is entirely personalized. Depending on how you are feeling at the moment, you can listen to music that is going to enhance your positive feelings.

3. Read something that interests you.

While resting your mind should be an objective, stimulating it with something that you find interesting is a great way to spend your me time. Whether it is an article that you have been meaning to read or a book you'd like to catch up on, enjoy yourself as you read.

If the writing is making you feel tired/drained/sad/moody, then you need to seek some different reading material. No one wants to spend their me time feeling their worst, so make sure that you do not set this up for yourself in this way.

4. Indulge in your favorite food or beverage.

Food is a very comforting aspect of life for a lot of people. It is a very valid thing for you to enjoy consuming the things that make you feel good or bring up great memories. When you spend this time alone, no distractions, it is a good chance to truly see what is going on in your head.

Some days, it might be harder than others to fully open up to yourself and settle down mentally. With the help of food that comforts you, your goal should be to work on this until you feel that you are able to be truly authentic with yourself.

5. Think positively before bed.

If you have never meditated before or if you do not see any appeal in meditating now, consider spending some time before you sleep on your positive intentions — these can be anything at all that you want to happen. They should all lead to a positive result, which is the most important part of the process.

Consider what you are grateful for and what you already have in abundance. Next, you can focus on the things that you still want. Envision them and imagine that you have them all. Know that these things are attainable for you if you continue to work hard and remain active on your quest to better your time.

Quick Start Action Step

If you do not see any free time on your schedule this week, plan for at least 10 minutes before bed each night that you are going to dedicate toward your me time. Getting ideas from the above steps, select an activity that you have been wanting to do for a while. Make sure that the reason you want to do it is that it benefits you.

Allow yourself some uninterrupted time to have this experience with yourself, paying attention to any of the feelings that rise to the surface in the process. You might realize that you are holding on to a lot more than you think. As you become more acquainted with yourself, it will be easier to think about things that you would truly like to do and experience.

Chapter 14: More Time Management Strategies

Chapter 14: More Time Management Strategies

As you work on these steps toward bettering your time management skills, your focus should be on getting results. While it can be practical to go through the motions of adopting these new habits and using these techniques, what will truly bring you results is a commitment to consistency. Know that these methods are meant to help you permanently, not only temporarily.

Batch Processing

Batch processing is a fairly easy concept to apply to various areas of your life. It is the idea that you can perform a single task that is going to benefit more than just one outcome. An example of this would be putting your bills on auto-pay. Instead of having to remember to pay each bill monthly, you would perform one action and then be finished with the task.

When you think about your life and what you are responsible for, it is likely that there are many opportunities to incorporate the batch processing technique into your schedule. Another example would be cooking meals in bulk so that you can eat dinner with your family and use that same food for packed lunches the next day. Thinking this way can save you a lot of time and energy. This is how you can apply batch processing to your own life:

1. Take note of the tasks you have each week that are repetitive. Some of these things will likely include driving to work/school/town, cooking, paying bills, caring for children, and more.

2. Think about ways that you can consolidate these tasks. If you notice that you are driving back and forth a lot, think about different routes that you can take that would make more sense and save you time. Join a carpool or get the kids to take the school bus. These small things can make a huge difference in the time that you have.

3. Use products that are meant for a two-in-one purpose. From shampoo and conditioner to household cleaning products, there are ways for you to shop smarter in order to save time. By doing this, you aren't cutting corners. You are simply getting to the same end result in less time.

4. Go to bigger stores that will have all that you need in one stop. If you can combine the act of grocery shopping with picking up household goods, then opt for the store that gives you this selection. You will feel satisfied knowing that you only have to stop at one place in order to get everything you need.

Making Blocks of Time

A self-explanatory strategy, it is a smart idea to create blocks of time in your schedule. While there are certain tasks that must be done at certain times, there are others in which you have the ability to dictate. Think carefully about the way that you do this because this is going to determine how much free time you have.

If you know that the kids are going to be busy with after-school activities and then immediately going to play at a friend's house, you can take these two blocks of time and turn them into one large block of free time for yourself. Alternatively, you can take the two blocks of time and devote them to cleaning up around the house while it is empty.

The freedom of doing whatever you would like with your blocks of time is the best part of this strategy. Depending on what kind of a week you are having, you can schedule it accordingly. Whenever you can, look for opportunities to make blocks of time in order to free up more time. Here is how you can accomplish this:

1. *Work when others are working.* This normally applies to the average job, but you will also want to plan on working around the house when the rest of the household is busy working too. For example, if your spouse is sprucing up the garage, take this time to work on some loads of laundry. When you are finished with this, you will be able to spend your free time together.

2. *Be as specific as you can.* Mark out all of the time blocks on your calendar so you are able to follow them clearly. Making time blocks requires a lot of thinking ahead and estimation. Make sure that you are giving yourself enough time to have a balance in your schedule.

3. *Remember to say no.* If a friend calls and asks

you if you'd like to go out yet you know that you have time blocked for working on tasks, it is going to take willpower to say no. If you had said yes, though, your time blocks would be spent on too much leisure time, feeling as though you have run out of working time. Saying no is meant to keep your life balanced.

Photographic Memory

A skill more than a strategy, utilizing your photographic memory can help you save time. Naturally, people think differently and remember things differently. Having a photographic memory means that you are able to see something visually and remember it in great detail.

There are ways that you can exercise your brain in order to enhance this skill. Remember, it is going to come naturally for some, but it could be harder for others. Be patient with yourself as you explore different ways in which to boost your photographic memory. These are some steps that you can take if you'd like to work on yours:

1. Think about a building or house that you

have access to and that you are familiar with. It can be your own home, the grocery store, or even your best friend's workplace. Close your eyes and visualize it for a few moments.

2. Take note of the things that stand out about the place and make it unique. These identifiers are going to help you remember it in its entirety. Are there stains on the ceiling? Is the furniture a bright color? Tap into these details.

3. Now, imagine that you are walking through the space. Pay attention to which side each item is on. What do you see as you walk straight through the rooms? Remember the unique details that you have just thought of. How and where do they fit in?

4. Once you have thoroughly done as many visual walkthroughs as you feel necessary, go to this place and see how well you have done. To become better at the process, try to look at something or someplace that you'd like to remember while being as focused as you can. Rid yourself of any distractions.

Accelerated Learning

The most advanced method of teaching and learning used today is accelerated learning. It allows you to engage your entire being in the process of learning something new. It incorporates your emotions, body, the process of creation, collaboration, senses, and visuals into one method.

When you fully immerse yourself in something that you would like to learn, it is found that you are able to retain the information better. This is exactly what accelerated learning aims to teach you. These are some examples of ways that you can apply accelerated learning into your own life:

1. Get enough sleep. Make sure that you are getting enough sleep before tackling any tasks on your schedule. When you do not get enough, both your mind and body are in jeopardy. Because both are required in order to apply accelerated learning, it won't be possible to retain this type of information if you are exhausted.

2. Allow yourself to see connections. While you might fill out charts regularly at work, stop and consider what the purpose of this action is. Does it clearly present information to your peers so that they are able to process it and pass it on? Know that all of your actions have a greater purpose.

3. *Keep your brain active.* Memorization is a great way to enhance your learning skills. Try to memorize a quote, poem, or song each week. It can be anything that interests you. This will allow you to give your brain some variety while also keeping it keen and strong.

4. *Take an immersive approach.* No matter what you are doing, fully immerse yourself into it. From work to free time, know that you are going to benefit more if you are truly present in each moment. Leave your worries about other things or distractions behind. This can take some practice, but the results you will see will motivate you to be more present in what you are doing.

Quick Start Action Step

Pick a strategy that you feel would work best in your life and apply it this week. Making sure that you follow the steps carefully, commit to it for at least a week and see what kind of a difference you notice in your life.

You are not obligated to do only one of these strategies. As you begin to see success, you can add other ones into your life to see if they also work for you. Use as many as you feel would be practical.

Chapter 15: Simplifying Your Life

Chapter 15: Simplifying Your Life

Taking a "less is more" approach to your life can create more time for you to utilize. When you focus on doing too much and having material possessions in abundance, it becomes easier to lose track of what you actually need to be focusing on.

When you have less, you also have less to worry about. It is a simple concept that allows you to focus on the things that are most important. It is another way to create balance and a better flow to the things that you do each day.

Benefits of Simplicity

The idea of living more simply might push you away because you do not want to part with the things that you love and enjoy. You don't have to do this in order to create simplicity. What you must do is act smarter about what you do and what you buy. This dictates what you spend your time on. Consider these benefits of living a simple lifestyle and consider how they can impact other aspects of your daily life:

1. *Getting better sleep:* As you know, sleep is a critical part of having a great day. You need sleep in order to function and in order to regulate your emotions. There is nothing good about making it through a day while feeling like you are barely holding on.

2. *Less stimulation:* When you live with less, there becomes less chance of becoming distracted. You do not have to part with all of your entertainment devices and methods, but you also do not have to hold on to multiple. Keeping your favorite ones will make the time you spend using them more enjoyable while also allowing you to focus when you need to.

3. *More creativity:* Those who have less use their imagination more. This is a great way to spend your time that can actually benefit you in many ways. When you are imaginative, you can come up with better solutions to problems. In turn, this also makes you happier. Creativity is a great motivational point to begin any task or to even spend your free time exploring.

4. *Decreased sensitivity:* The more that you experience, the more energy you are at risk of taking on. For example, if you are watching TV while listening to music, your mood and emotions will be impacted by each of these things. It can become complicated when you are watching a sad movie and listening to a happy song at the same time. This subtle conflict influences your subconscious more than you think. When you have less of this around you, your sensitivity sees a noticeable decrease.

5. *Environmental protection:* When you have less, you also have less waste. This is something to consider when you think of the overall environmental picture. Your carbon footprint in this world is important, just as everyone else's is. By living simply, you are doing your part to reduce the level of output that you are creating, and that is a beautiful thing.

6. *Improved relationships:* Focusing less on things gives you more time to focus on people. When you feel guilty for not spending enough time with those you love, it is probably because you feel that other things are taking up your time. As you become better with scheduling, you will have the ability to redeem this time. A simple life means that you will have no problem focusing on the people in front of you. Not only will your loved ones appreciate this, but your bonds will also begin to grow.

Steps to Take

While there isn't a standard way for you to apply simplistic concepts into your life, there are many steps that you can take that will get you there. All of the following steps hold the same weight of value to them. You don't have to worry about completing them all at once or in the order that they are stated. As long as you make an effort to change something in each of these aspects of your life, you will be able to see a noticeable difference:

1. Utilize one form of entertainment at a time. While there are so many things that you probably enjoy doing for fun, remember that overstimulation can actually end up stressing you out. If you find that you are having a good time, there is no need to add anything else into what you are doing. Be present in that activity and enjoy yourself.

2. Declutter your home. Working up the time and energy to declutter can be a struggle, but it is something that is worthwhile. You will feel so much more at ease knowing where all of your belongings are. Get rid of the things that no longer serve you, and pass them along to others who can use them right now. You will feel great about coming home to a simplified home.

3. *Donate your time.* Volunteer work is a great way to be reminded of simplicity. You can apply what you learn during your volunteering toward your own lifestyle. Being mindful of all that you currently have allows you to see that you do not *need* everything that you possess. Some things are luxuries, and your life isn't going to stop just because you have less of them.

4. *Focus on your spirituality.* While this has nothing to do with religion and more to do with what you truly believe in, take some time to pay attention to your morals. These are what make you who you are. Learn how to apply your actions toward behaviors that align with these morals. This is how to stay true to yourself, and this is one of the most basic actions that you can take toward simplicity.

5. *Get rid of what makes you unhappy.* This sounds like a no-brainer, but it is actually more difficult than you think. As humans, we are resilient. There are probably several things in your life right now that you are tolerating when you can actually just remove or resolve them in order to continue moving forward. Take a look at what isn't working or what is clashing. You will be able to get to the root of the problem and then make an effort to simplify it.

Quick Start Action Step

Commit to a day where you plan on decluttering your home. You do not need to focus on this task for an entire day, but you will need at least a few solid hours of work. As soon as you are able to complete your first big decluttering effort, any future cleaning is going to be a lot easier for you.

Make piles for your items. You should have one that is designated for trash or things that no longer work. These are the items that you cannot reuse or repurpose in any way. Getting rid of these is going to create a lot more space for organization or new items to replace them if necessary.

You should have a "donate" pile. Items that go in this

pile still have a usable function to them, yet they no longer serve you or your life. These things can be donated or re-gifted to people who you feel will have a better use for them. Consider putting items in this pile that you have not used for more than three months. If an entire season has passed without you utilizing it, then you likely do not need it.

The last pile is the one where your belongings go. You can put them here while you sort through the rest of the items. Once you finish the sorting process, you will then be able to organize everything to your liking. Being able to find exactly what you are looking for when you need it is a great feeling.

In order to avoid future clutter, make sure that you are only purchasing items that you need. Always remember to put your belongings back where they go, and take pride in the fact that you worked so hard on getting organized.

This action is going to take a lot of willpower because no one can force you to do it. Tap into your self-discipline and remind yourself about how great you will feel when you have a simple lifestyle.

BONUS Chapter: Managing Time with the Family

BONUS Chapter: Managing Time with the Family

Family is an important aspect of every working mother's life. Being able to spend time with the ones that you are closest to is a great way for you to unwind after dealing with a busy day full of tasks. It becomes a struggle when you feel that your schedule is too busy to accommodate the time that you wish you could spend with your family.

By now, you have realized that there are several strategies that you can use to make more time. Having free time to spend with your family isn't much to ask for at all. Know that you and your loved ones deserve to have this time together, no matter how busy you become.

Keeping your values in mind will help remind you to make time for your family. If you value the time spent together, it will serve as a constant reminder to keep pushing forward so that you can be rewarded with this bonding time.

You do not have to all sit around the house in order to

spend quality time with one another. Think about all that there is to do, both from home and outside of the home. Going out with your family is a great use of your time, and it can also serve other purposes.

If you have errands to run, running them together is a way to still have company while also completing your tasks. You can also bring your family along for errands while also doing something fun afterward. There are many ways that you can utilize time blocking in order to make sure that you have enough balance with your family.

No matter what you decide to do, it makes a noticeable difference in your mood and your mindset when you are able to share this time together. Being with your family can make the time you spend working a lot less difficult. Consider these benefits as you prioritize your time:

1. Less stress: Simply being in the company of the ones you love has the ability to turn your mood around. Whether you have had a bad day or were too busy to stop and think, being with your family can reduce your stress levels. As you know, this is very important to stay on top of your time management.

Stress is something that can make you lose track of time.

2. *More fun:* It is important that you have fun every day. Never forget that you need to make room for fun in your life. While certain things require seriousness, you do not need to remain in this state of being during your free time. Being with your family allows you the chance to be your total self. Let yourself have fun, and try to let go of all the thoughts that worry you that you might be holding on to.

3. *Strengthening bonds:* While your spouse and children might see a lot of you around the house in passing, this does not mean that you are truly bonding. A lot of families consider this as time spent together when it is merely just time spent existing under the same roof. Be mindful of this, and try to have real conversations and deep connections with your family. The bonds that you create will have the ability to build you up.

4. *Having support:* When you are close to your family, it is like you have an automatic support system to be there for you with everything that you do. This is important when you are trying to improve your time management skills because their support can act as a motivation for you. It is always nice to know that your family believes in you and vice versa.

5. *Discussing fears:* We all have them, yet we seldom talk about our fears. It is an honest action that should happen more often. Your fears can stop you from going after what you want because they will trick you into believing that you aren't good enough. If you have ever felt this way, you know how good it feels to admit your deepest thoughts to someone. Spending time with your family gives you this chance to have real, honest talks.

Steps to Take

As you work on your journey to becoming great with time management, there are still ways for you to improve your relationships with your family simultaneously. These are some steps that you can follow to ensure that you are keeping a great balance between family time and other time:

1. *Have family meetings.* Regular family meetings give each person a chance to be heard. You can decide on activities that you would like to do together or discuss issues that you might be going through. Regular communication is a great way to become closer to one another.

You can also delegate tasks during these meetings. This is your chance to assign tasks and talk about goals. Implementing a rewards system is also a great way to motivate each other to get more done around the house.

2. *Share a calendar.* In order for everyone in the household to be on the same page, utilizing a family calendar is a great idea. Whether you prefer it to be physical, digital, or both, make sure that each person has their own access to it with the ability to add/remove events.

When you all know what to expect from the week ahead, it makes it a lot easier to plan when you are going to be able to spend time together. It also creates a sense of inclusivity when you share a calendar with your loved ones.

3. *Hold game nights.* A fun way to spend time together is to hold a regular family game night. It does not need to be anything formal, but all you need to do is schedule a time when everyone is free for a few hours. Take turns picking board games to play, and have snacks and drinks around the table.

Game nights are a great bonding experience for everyone to participate in. No matter what kind of day you all had, you can come together and let go of any negativity by playing these games and having fun.

4. *Do chores together.* Chores are an inevitable part of any household. While it might be in your nature to take them on yourself, it is not only a mother's responsibility. Get your children and spouse involved by distributing the chores that must be done each week.

You can create a chart to indicate who is responsible for what. If you have younger children, using a rewards system for the incentive is normally successful. Doing chores together is another way to come together as a family while also serving a productive cause.

5. *Learn routines.* You are all individuals with different obligations and interests. To show that you care about one another, be mindful of everyone's routines. From the time spent getting ready each morning to responsibilities outside of the home, knowing what your family is up to can help to establish when you can spend time together.

There is nothing worse than a family living together yet never knowing where anyone is or what they are doing. Communication is essential for keeping up with one another. A simple text or call can do a lot to help one another figure out how each schedule is going to mesh together.

Quick Start Action Step

Schedule one family activity this week. Whether you would like to hold a game night or go out to see a movie, make sure that you can reference your calendar and decide on a time that works best for all of you. Come together to select an activity that you would all enjoy.

A great idea is to write down activities that you can do together and place them in a jar. When you have time to spend with one another, you can take turns selecting a paper that will tell you which activity you should do. This is a fun and quick way to spend time together.

You can start by scheduling one family activity a week, but you will soon realize that it is going to be a lot easier than you think to make time for family fun. Aim to increase the frequency, trying to plan more time together as the weeks progress.

Time spent with your family is so special because it is time spent with the people that see you at your highest and lowest points. This is a unique bond that is important to keep as strong as you can. Having the support of your family can get you through some of the worst times that you will experience.

Conclusion

By reading through all of the different steps that you can take to ensure that you are making the best use of your time, you will realize that time is actually very flexible. While you cannot change the obligations that you have, you can change your approach to dealing with them. As you make smart scheduling decisions, you will realize that you do have free time to spare.

While you might not be able to create more time at the snap of a finger, you do have the ability to prioritize the things that are important to you. When you have the motivation to do these things, there is a renewed energy that will kick in to help you. Feeling capable of completing your tasks that have deadlines, you will find your way to the things that you desire most as quickly and stress-free as possible.

Changing your perspective has a great deal to do with your time management skills. If you settle into negative thinking and believing that you will never have any time for yourself, then this becomes your reality. Keeping your mindset positive is going to take your farther than wallowing in the false promise that there is never going to be any free time to take.

Busy women juggle a lot all at once. From keeping up with your children to bonding with your spouse, making sure your career is flourishing, and being the best homemaker that you can, it is no wonder that there are times when you feel spent. By utilizing the techniques provided, you will be able to feel accomplished and proud of yourself.

Instead of worrying about how you are going to fit everything into your schedule, you are going to stay one step ahead. Becoming a master as scheduling, prioritizing, and time blocking, you will come to realize that you can do anything you truly want to. All of this can be accomplished while still ensuring that there is time for you to rest.

You do not have to give up on your free time or time spent with your loved ones in order to complete your pressing tasks. This is counterproductive, as it only burns you out faster. By listening to your mind and body, you will be able to determine what you need more of in order to stay happy. Listening to yourself is important; without your health, you won't be able to get anything done.

You will experience some setbacks — everyone does. When you are trying something new, it is natural for you to want to revert to your old ways. This might involve procrastination, the most common time killer that there is. Do not punish yourself if this happens. The only thing that you can do is commit to moving forward. Think about ways that you can do better and be better. Try to go over the tips that will help you with avoiding procrastination and feeling motivated to do your best.

By creating new habits for yourself, you are going to stay on top of your time management skills that you have learned. These aren't only temporary suggestions to get you by for the week. They are real-life solutions that you can use permanently. As long as you are able to stay motivated and set your priorities, then you will be able to hold these lifelong habits that will assist you with managing your time.

When you learn how to get a great start to your day, you will be guaranteed productivity. Never underestimate a great night's sleep and a nutritious breakfast meal. Both will get you on the right track toward accomplishment and motivation. Make sure that you prioritize your mornings, sticking to a morning routine that allows you to complete everything without having to rush out the door.

As you navigate through your schedule and learn about the tasks you have for your upcoming week, do not let them intimidate you. Believe that you are a strong and powerful woman who is able to accomplish anything that you put your mind to. The steps provided to you will allow you to become stronger and more confident each day that you use them.

References

Cobb, J. (2019, May 13). 5 practices to prime accelerated learning. Retrieved from https://www.missiontolearn.com/accelerated-learning-techniques/

Conti, G. (2017, July 11). A guide to delegating tasks effectively (and why you should). Retrieved from https://www.meistertask.com/blog/delegate-tasks-effectively/

Cooper, B. (2019, February 26). Beyond time management: why we really procrastinate and how to finally stop - ambition & balance. Retrieved from https://doist.com/blog/strategies-for-overcoming-procrastination/

How to develop a photographic memory: 4 easy steps — barking up the wrong tree. (2018, October

2). Retrieved from
https://www.bakadesuyo.com/2013/10/how-to-develop-a-photographic-memory/

Huber, L. (2019, August 26). 7 ways to level up your mindset. Retrieved from
https://medium.com/swlh/7-ways-to-level-up-your-mindset-5395fd103310

Keith, K. (2015, May 19). Time management stats that may surprise you. Retrieved from
https://www.cornerstonedynamics.com/time-management-stats-that-may-surprise-you/

Konigsberg, R. (2014, August 29). Time management techniques for the modern woman. Retrieved from https://www.realsimple.com/work-life/life-strategies/time-management/time-management-techniques?slide=2055

Mariama-Arthur, K. (2017, February 24). Why mindset mastery is vital to your success. Retrieved from
https://www.entrepreneur.com/article/285466

Miller, C. (2015, November 4). Stressed, tired, rushed:

a portrait of the modern family. Retrieved from
https://www.nytimes.com/2015/11/05/upshot
/stressed-tired-rushed-a-portrait-of-the-
modern-family.html

Moland, T. (2011, December 30). Time management
for the family. Retrieved from
https://www.canadianliving.com/life-and-
relationships/family/article/time-
management-for-the-family

Purewal, D. (2017, November 29). 7 benefits of me
time. Retrieved from
https://www.clairebuck.com/benefits-of-me-
time/

Reddy, C. (2019, June 28). Time management for
working women: 14 tips and secrets. Retrieved
from https://content.wisestep.com/time-
management-for-working-women-tips-and-
secrets/

Rosselit, B. (2015, July 27). 10 reasons why a simple
lifestyle reduces stress and benefits your
health. Retrieved from
https://www.lifehack.org/276972/10-reasons-
why-simple-lifestyle-reduces-stress-and-

benefits-your-health

Runyan, A. (2017, March 16). 13 time management habits of successful women. Retrieved from https://www.classycareergirl.com/2015/09/my-13-time-management-and-productivity-principles-for-dream-career-launchers/

Taylor, H. (2019, September 10). History of time management. Retrieved from https://www.taylorintime.com/history-of-time-management/

The top 12 time management apps and tools. (2018, July 4). Retrieved from https://www.spadetechnology.com/the-top-12-time-management-apps-and-tools/

Vooijs, M. (2017, September 29). Time management: The amazing benefits of an early start. Retrieved from https://www.thehospitalitist.nl/geen-categorie/time-management-the-amazing-benefits-of-an-early-start/

Young, S. (2018b, January 30). 18 tricks to make new habits stick. Retrieved from https://www.lifehack.org/articles/featured/18-tricks-to-make-new-habits-stick.html

benefits-your-health

Runyan, A. (2017, March 16). 13 time management habits of successful women. Retrieved from https://www.classycareergirl.com/2015/09/my-13-time-management-and-productivity-principles-for-dream-career-launchers/

Taylor, H. (2019, September 10). History of time management. Retrieved from https://www.taylorintime.com/history-of-time-management/

The top 12 time management apps and tools. (2018, July 4). Retrieved from https://www.spadetechnology.com/the-top-12-time-management-apps-and-tools/

Vooijs, M. (2017, September 29). Time management: The amazing benefits of an early start. Retrieved from https://www.thehospitalitist.nl/geen-categorie/time-management-the-amazing-benefits-of-an-early-start/

Young, S. (2018b, January 30). 18 tricks to make new habits stick. Retrieved from https://www.lifehack.org/articles/featured/18-tricks-to-make-new-habits-stick.html